THE LITTL

Ken Cooper studied enginec   ,......g
the RAF at the beginning of World War II. After
a flying accident he became an infantryman and
served with the regular Army until 1959. He
married in 1945, and he and his wife, a QA
nursing sister, served together in the Far East,
Middle East and Western Europe. They enjoyed
travelling in desert and mountain terrain and have
climbed together in the Himalayas as well as many
other ranges. Retired in 1984, they now live in
Oxfordshire.

© *K. W. Cooper 1973*
First published in Great Britain 1973
First paperback edition 1992

ISBN 0 7090 4710 X

Robert Hale Limited
Clerkenwell House
Clerkenwell Green
London EC1R 0HT

The right of K. W. Cooper to be identified as author
of this work has been asserted by him in accordance
with the Copyright, Designs and Patents Act 1988.

Printed in Great Britain by
St Edmundsbury Press Limited, Bury St Edmunds, Suffolk.
Bound by WBC Bookbinders Limited.

THE LITTLE MEN

K. W. COOPER

ROBERT HALE · LONDON

CONTENTS

ILLUSTRATIONS

Between pages 96 and 97

ONE

Up the Ukhrul Track

In Calcutta an old yellow open taxi whisked me through streets packed with sweating humanity and deposited me at the Grand Hotel. My room was already occupied by five other officers sleeping under the slowly revolving fan, in various states of undress. I limped downstairs into the late afternoon. Outside in Chowringhee, little Indian kids were touting useless junk – newspapers, watches, rings and coloured postcards of the city. It was the spring of 1944. I had been sent down on sick leave from Base Hospital on the Burma border.

At first, the sights and sounds of civilisation made my thoughts quicken with excitement. American airmen walked by with fat buttocks tight against the satin sheen of their drill trousers, followed by barefoot urchins crying:

"*Buck sheesh*, sahib: no mamma, no pappa, *buck sheesh*, sahib."

I went a long way up towards the fort. Rickshaw boys followed me up the street, touting:

"Rickshaw, sahib? Where you go? Saturday Club? Firpo? Good rickshaw, sahib."

I was bored and indecisive. An ancient cab drew up with an even more ancient Sikh at the wheel. He raised his eyebrows slightly.

"You want *pukka* place, sahib, good girl, white university student, plenty good, only officer, sahib?" I climbed into the cab.

"Turn this bloody thing round – *peechy abhi*, Grand Hotel *ko jao*."

The Sikh cursed me under his breath and honked his way back along the darkening street.

Ten days later I was back in Comilla to catch a plane for Imphal. I arranged to meet Sister F. at the officer's club. She looked well and lovely as ever. We danced to the accompaniment of an ancient gramophone. When it was time to go, I took her back to the hospital and we said our goodbyes in the moonlight.

"Do you think," I asked, "that we will ever meet again?"

"You know we will", she whispered in reply, "you know we will."

Understandably, the amenities at Comilla appealed to me no end, and I was loath to leave them behind.

It was barely light when I found myself airborne, bumping and yawing over the Manipur mountains. Gazing sleepily down at the carpet of green cloaking the wrinkled face of the hills, I shuddered slightly. Those trackless jungle-clad peaks down there seemed to me the most uncharitable places on earth at that moment.

At Imphal I learned that the battalion to which I had been posted had come back from the Tamu road front and were now in position astride the Ukhrul Road to the east of the town.

A bluff, friendly sergeant, driving an American 'Doodle-bug' truck had been sent to meet me.

"You the reinforcement officer for our mob, sir?"

I nodded, returning his searching stare:

"You're lucky," he went on breezily, and without bothering to salute. "It's cushy up where we are now – you've missed the worst part. You should have been down Tamu way with us. That was a right bastard, that was."

Putting on a suitably impressed and deferential face I settled myself in the cab of the truck.

The sergeant let in the gear with a loud clatter:

"Hold tight, sir. Sit back and enjoy the ride – it's a wonderful view, I don't think!"

He sounded like a courier on a coach trip to the Swallow Falls!

I had already been treated to numerous vivid descriptions of the most recent fighting, while in the Reinforcement Camp in Comilla. My companion on the drive up the Ukhrul track filled in the lurid details.

Early in March, when the Japanese had first begun their attempt to invade India, the 2nd Battalion of the Border Regiment had been "right at the point of the sharp-end". That was how the sergeant put it to me. The 20th Indian Division had been holding the approaches to Imphal at the southern end of the Kabaw valley:

We are the little men grown huge with death.
Stolid in squads or grumbling on fatigues
We held the honour of the regiment
And stifled our antipathies
Stiff-backed and parrot-wise with pamphlet learning
We officiated at the slaughter of the riverine peoples . . .

And all the good lads there that died for luck.

Alun Lewis

PREFACE

The Irrawaddy river is immensely wide; wide and shining and the colour of the sky, which, in the translucent heat, becomes one with the wild greenness and the shimmering sand of the farther shore.

Villages straggle along the river's banks, their ramshackle bamboo buildings half hidden among the trees on the low cliffs of white dust above the water's edge. The villages are cool oases of toddy palms, thatch and plantains, amid scorched paddyfields on the edge of a vast purple plain.

Sometimes I think about the river and its cool, perfumed villages: scarlet lilies from the flame trees litter the dust, and copper-smith birds knock-knock ceaselessly in time with the flickering mind-pictures. The utter stillness of sun-down comes back to me, and the call of the tuck-too lizard. Tuck-too! Tuck-too! Far away, the snarling pariah dogs wail and shriek to a rising moon. Pagodas float wraith-like amongst swaying palm fronds; their golden roofs hung with crystal bells tinkle a mad requiem in the gentle evening breeze.

The scene changes constantly. I remember lotus pools battered by monsoon torrents; blue mountains; high jungle grasses whispering in a dawn wind; tribesmen from the hills; monasteries; Buddhist shrines of wood, devilishly carved, beside rutted bullock-tracks. I see half forgotten faces of friends long dead; I hear snatches of their songs, and the sound of their columns marching through eerie, scented nights. It is a lower world region of memory between heaven and hades. Vague and remote, like a dream . . .

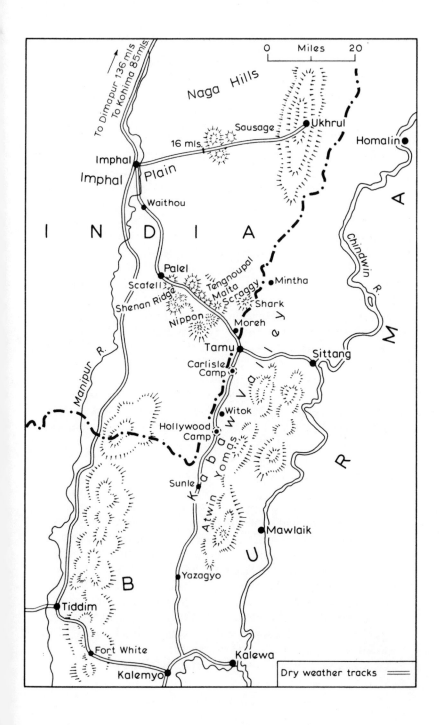

"Playing bloody football in the paddyfields in front of the perimeter we were, sir, and doing a bit of patrolling like."

One of the Border NCOs, a Corporal George, with his patrol had
knocked off a Japanese staff car, and got away with some papers
which turned out to contain the strength and dispositions of all the
enemy units facing the 20th Division. George had received an
immediate award of the Distinguished Conduct Medal.

Later, when the Division was withdrawing under orders, the battalion, together with the 4th/10th Gurkhas, had been ambushed on
a jungle track. In the confusion a bugler, Private Lennon, had
blown the regimental call, followed by the 'charge'. Thereupon
some of the Border men, led by Company Sergeant Major Lead-
bitter, had fallen upon the Japs with bayonets and driven them off.

Later still, when the same column was falling back even further,
the enemy had outflanked it once again and succeeded on this occasion in so disorganising the brigade group that it had been split up
into numerous small parties. Some of these took as long as a week
to rejoin the Brigade at a pre-arranged rendezvous. When the Battalion has taken up a defensive position in the Tengnoupal area,
they were on mountain peaks of 5,000 feet, the slopes of which were
covered in elephant grass and jungle. The summits of these hills, on
which the companies were dug in, were joined to one another by
narrow ridges forming saddles between the peaks. All water was
carried on the backs of the men up these precipitous slopes and
along the saddles to the trenches.

One particular fight which seemed indelibly stamped on the
sergeant's memory, he referred to as "that fukkin' duffy on Nippon
Hill".

One platoon had held Nippon Hill at first. When the Japs over-
ran it, the Battalion had spent five or six days on piecemeal attacks,
using platoons. Once or twice even single sections had tried to infil-
trate amongst the Jap bunker positions without success. Finally a
series of company assaults had been launched, all with the same
outcome – bloody repulse. The enemy had dug themselves in like
moles – right in and under the summit peak of Nippon Hill.

"By Christ, them little bastards can dig. They're underground
before our blokes have stopped spitting on their bloody 'ands"

The sergeant spoke in staccato bursts of feeling.

"Do you know, sir, the whole bloomin' battalion of the 3rd/1st

Gurkhas went up in one bloody great bash, and they couldn't get to the top of Nippon either. I wouldn't mind bettin' them same little bleedin' Japs are still on Nippon Hill next Christmas."

The Battalion had been relieved by troops of the 80th Brigade in early April. Pulling back almost to the edge of the Imphal plain, it had the task of preventing the Japs from gaining access should they succeed in outflanking 80th Brigade on the Tengnoupal Ridge.

As the battle for the passes built up to a climax, the Battalion went once more into forward positions on the Shenan Ridge. Here another ferocious 'duffy' had occurred on 'Scraggy Hill'.

With his description of the system of strong-points which ran 30 feet below the peak of Scraggy, the sergeant surpassed himself. Many of the forward posts had been overrun by the Japs, leaving a no-man's-land of not much more than ten or twenty yards. This had made digging impossible, and the men nearest the enemy were barely two feet underground, until mortar boxes filled with earth were brought up at night to provide the extra cover. Wiring was impossible and sanitation non-existent: dead lay everywhere in heaps in varying stages of decomposition.

"If you can imagine men having to plug their noses and breathe through their mouths because of the bloody smell, you'll have an idea how bad it was."

The sergeant held his nose between his forefingers and thumb in a gesture of utter disgust.

"When the Gurkhas relieved our lads, sir, their CO commandeered all the fags he could get his hands on, so his Johnnies could smoke all the time – even the Gurks couldn't stand the stench!"

Apparently the men in the forward position had been relieved every half hour. The strain was that bad.

Scraggy Hill seemed to fit the sergeant's idea of what some of the First World War battlefields had been like. Broken tree stumps, the ground scarred by trenches and pock-marked by shell holes, with vegetation obliterated from the ridge crests . . .

At this point we arrived near the perimeter of the 100th Brigade HQ where the sergeant had some errand or other.

It was almost dark when I finally reached Battalion HQ, somewhere near Milestone 16 . . . I was quickly seen by the Adjutant, David Kitchen, who gave me a cursory briefing. 'A' Company were on the left or west of the road on a sausage-shaped feature. 'B'

Company were forward of Battalion HQ on a saddle in the hills. 'C' Company were on 'Buttress' to the east of the road, with 'D' Company holding 'Beacon' further forward on the west side. A spot height on the map near 'D' Company's position, marked 4241, meant that the trenches up there were almost a thousand feet higher than the summit of Snowdon.

I heard the sound of shell-fire all the way up the road from Imphal, but here close to the front line, with the forward positions under bombardment, the noise had become suddenly infinitely more menacing. The whole area was waterlogged, and thunder clouds cloaked the forest-covered hills. The monsoon had begun a week or two earlier in all its uncomfortable severity.

My first night near Battalion HQ was startling. There were distant flashes, followed by dull reports, and every now and then a hastening whirrr . . . which seemed only feet overhead. Almost immediately followed the deafening slap and crash of exploding shells. The impersonal whine and crunch of the howling missiles, coming from out of nowhere, left me trembling and in a cold sweat, although the night air was clammy and hot.

My first impression of my Company was that I had arrived at an awkward time. There was an air of urgency, not to say confusion, in the proceedings. I hoped sincerely that everyone else knew what they were about. Personally I felt almost in the way, and now and then unwanted. Who the heck was where, doing what, was a mystery no one took the trouble to unravel for me at first. I spent a great deal of time helping to improve the defences in clinging mud, with the visibility often down to fifty yards; visiting sentry posts in torrential rain; listening to the men, and trying to sleep in water-logged dug-outs. The sounds of bursting mortar bombs and machine-gun fire made a constant accompaniment to the ceaseless downpour of the monsoon.

When someone found time to put me in the picture, I learned that the overall plan for the Fourteenth Army was a counter offensive. The XXXIII Corps was supposed to be pushing down from Kohima towards Imphal with one of its divisions, the 7th Indian, well out to the east of the road. The object was to get onto the enemy's flank as they advanced from Ukhrul. Our Corps, the IV, was mounting operations to break the Japanese cordon around Imphal, and in particular to break a way through to XXXIII Corps, coming down from Kohima. The 20th Indian Division had the task of breaking out eastwards towards Ukhrul itself.

In the meantime it had become increasingly obvious that the enemy had some unfinished plans of his own . . . Within days 'A' Company, on 'Sausage', were cut off completely and surrounded by fanatical Japanese infantry. Several bloody attempts were made to reach the company without success. Eventually they were supplied entirely from the air through the roof of the jungle. Unfortunately many air drops, frustrated by the weather conditions, resulted in food and ammunition falling between our own troops and the Japanese. Both sides fought for possession of it.

Climbing up to company positions took four or five hours from Battalion HQ, and left you without breath in your body or strength in your limbs. If the mist had cleared and the clouds dispersed momentarily, while you were on top, you could see perhaps for fifty miles. The green wilderness went on for ever, it seemed, all dead and still and silent.

The events of the next week or two are blurred, almost without sequence in my mind. I was left with vivid nightmare pictures of walking wounded – ragged men, carrying their weapons and little else, hobbling and sliding and cursing towards the Regimental Aid Post; of the half light dawn, beneath dripping trees, with the wounded huddled in groups under sodden blankets or lying, heads in the mud, torn and gashed with appalling injuries, some already turning gangrenous in the festering conditions.

In a final all-out attempt to get down the road and into Imphal itself, the Japs finally outflanked the Battalion and attacked Brigade HQ itself. Utter chaos ensued, and the wounded were hit again and again. Everyone – cooks, mule-drivers, staff officers and anyone who could – took up the weapons of the dead and fought where they stood. Dug-in tanks blasted the ferocious enemy attacks over open sights with high explosives and smashed their quickly constructed bunkers with solid shot. Extreme fatigue assailed everyone. There were some men going mad with fever and the strain of the hellish conditions.

On patrol amid tall, dripping jungle and dark menacing shadows, we heard the cries and screams of enemy wounded. In one clearing, not far from the Company positions, there was a lotus pool, blasted by the monsoon torrent: it was full of Jap

corpses rotting, emaciated yellow hands clutching at the empty
sky. Parachutes, hundreds of them, hung from the top-most
branches of the trees. The scenes were repeated, while the days
stood still.

In a lull the dead were buried. The shallow graves filled with
water as quickly as they were dug. The work went on endlessly.
Flash floods collapsed the trenches again and again.

After fifteen days the wounded were brought down from 'A'
Company. Some of the earlier wounded had drowned in their own
trenches. The survivors lay in the open in the unrelenting rain, half
naked, mud-splattered, smelling of rotting vegetation. Ulcerous
wounds exposed limbs to the white of bone.

The battle resolved itself into a personal problem of survival, an
exhausting, unremitting struggle with nature itself; with mud and
mosquitoes and disease; with the awful loneliness of a lost world
under a dripping desolation of sodden foliage . . .

Thirty-seven days after the Battalion had taken up its position on
that 'quiet sector' astride the Imphal – Ukhrul road, the Japanese
offensive petered out.

For the first time, after five months of ordered, planned withdrawal and standing fast in bloody battles of attrition, the 20th
Division at last moved forward. Marching eastwards towards
Ukhrul, the Battalion saw evidence of the Japanese everywhere –
discarded equipment, guns, corpses and burnt-out vehicles. All the
debris of a retreating army. And once the awful evidence of the
enemy's barbarity – the body of a British officer nailed to a tree
with Japanese bayonets. The story had got around, however, that
this atrocity was the work of Jifs, as the small force of Indian traitors was called.

Somewhere near Kasom, about the middle of July, the Battalion
was halted, loaded onto transport, and brought back down the
rutted track in jolting convoy. To Imphal? No such luck – but
through and on south six miles towards Palel.

Beside the track which borders the lifeless waters of the Waithou
lake the Battalion debussed and looked around. A bleak hillside,
strewn with refuse and scarred with filthy trenches, reared its unin-
viting bulk into the glowering storm clouds. And there the
Battalion sat out the rains.

TWO

The Platoon

Before long the incredibly steep and muddy hillside, which had become our new home above the Palel track, resembled a shanty town. Tents, tarpaulins, bits of corrugated tin and bamboo huts covered the holes and dug-outs which held our bivouacs. We even carried stones to place neatly round the Battalion HQ tent and the Company 'offices', and down on the track we fixed a tall pole on which the dragon standard was flown proudly.

Narrow footpaths wound around the gradient of the mountain-side. Great hollows were dug into the side of the hill and covered with flapping bleached canvas for use as officers' and sergeants' mess tents. We officers slept in slots cut back beneath the earth, and such things as camp beds, folding chairs, blankets and various other luxuries began to appear from the rear.

From the camp one could see for miles across a sea of furrowed summits, rising so far away that the jungle trees took on the appearance of a velvety green carpet. Down below, the shoreline of the lake stretched around the misty waters to more hills where other battalions were likewise camped.

In the mornings we could hear the mournful sounds of the Gurkha bagpipes drifting through the clammy, silent air.

At nightfall, as the sun sank blood-red over the hazy distant peaks, we would hear the pipes again and the chorus of bugles calling across the wilderness.

There were moments in those evenings of strange beauty, coupled with a sense of isolation, which filled one with sadness and nostalgia.

A week or two followed, during which many of the men got leave to India. The Viceroy, Field-Marshal Wavell, came up and presented decorations and awards to the Brigade, and close on his heels 'Supremo' himself, Lord Louis Mountbatten. In his inimitable way he climbed onto a ration box (which just happened to be there for the purpose) and, calling everyone around him, he addressed us in his breezy Naval manner, congratulating us for the way the Battalion had conducted itself in the defence of the Imphal plain. After that, we had a month or so to digest the lessons learnt in the campaign, and I was given the job of training reinforcement NCOs for the future.

About this time I had the good fortune to be sent to Imphal on a short course, which was, in fact, only an excuse to allow some of us a three-day rest in a back area, where we could see the odd open-air film show and enjoy a bath and drink at the officers' club.

When the Battalion had arrived in Waithou beside the lake, my own platoon had been a little more than a handful of men. Now both they and the fellows who had joined recently had begun to appear as entities – to have personalities and peculiarities. As time went on we began to build up a family spirit.

I could devote pages to these men, who have always remained in my memory more clearly than the hundreds of soldiers with whom I have served since those days. As it is, I must content myself with a word or two about some of them.

My platoon headquarters consisted of Lance-Sergeant Woods and Sergeant Florence, my batman Smith, Morrisroe the runner, and Bullard and Lawson, the 2-inch mortar team.

The sergeants were both rather quiet and sincere men. Born leaders, they fussed over the welfare of the platoon like mother hens. 'Lakri'* Woods was a Lancastrian with a broad accent, he had received wounds and a Military Medal in the recent campaign and was destined to receive both again in the next.

Dick Florence was Welsh and had the temperament of the Celtic race in full measure. For Smith, the war was a very serious business. Short and wrinkled, with sun-blackened skin, he could have passed easily for a native; in fact he was a Mancunian. He gave me the most unstinting, devoted loyalty and faithful service that ever one man gave another. He was the bravest of the brave. I became very fond of him. A life-long friendship was formed in those times.

* The Hindustani word for 'sticks'.

'Bull' Bullard was the platoon tough and Cockney clown. When the war ended he had fought in practically every engagement in which the Battalion took part, and seemed indestructible.

Jock Lawson, the other 2-inch mortar man, was a canny Scot, a thinker with wise ways and a terrible temper when roused. He was a fine soldier, and was destined to lead others on patrols without benefit of military rank, for he was a very private, private soldier, and never gave his services lightly.

Ernie Morrisroe, the runner, was . . . well, what can one say about a man who carried imperative messages across bullet-swept ground with his hands in his pockets and a fag in his mouth? Mad! No, brave as hell. Though scared as the rest of us, he never showed it.

Amongst the others in the platoon was a bren-gunner named 'Tish' Isherwood, with a raucous sense of humour and the unfailing high spirits and grit of the best type of Yorkshireman.

Private Andy Thomas, a tearaway Liverpool Welshman, was another stalwart, and his 'mucker', Barrett, handled grenades like cricket balls.

Billy Hughes was a true border man from Maryport in Cumberland. A section corporal, he was a fine, willing fellow with a cheerful smile, always ready to carry out unquestioningly the many difficult and dangerous tasks set for him. Like all men of integrity, he took much more than his share of the rough end of the stick and never once let any of us down.

Reid was getting on for 45 years old; how he ever found his way into a rifle platoon I cannot imagine, and he never seemed quite to accustom himself to life in the company of a band of ruthless young thugs. We ribbed him and called him 'Pop', but he somehow managed to keep up and did whatever was required of him. The average age of the platoon was perhaps 25 or 26.

When the Battalion was ordered forward once again, my platoon was still well under strength, as were most of the other platoons. The war establishment was then supposed to be over forty: my platoon mustered 28 NCOs and men.

Robin Gordon, a sheep farmer from New Zealand with whom I had become friendly when we had joined a battalion of Gurkhas by some error of Indian administration had, like myself, found his rightful regiment and become the Assault Pioneer Platoon

Commander. When our duties permitted we would go off together and drink rum and water in the privacy of our bivouacs, and talk about everything under the sun but soldiering.

John Margarson, Charlie Bates and Tommy Turner, three of the other platoon commanders, often joined Robin and me in these sessions; but Johnny always refused the rum in case it slowed his reflexes – he was determined to survive the war and marry his sweetheart.

Soon, our rest and training completed, we prepared for the move back into action.

All stores, camp-beds, chairs – in fact all superfluous gear – were sent back to our Admin. Company at Imphal, and once more we slept on the ground, fed with our platoons and lived in our equipment, weapons at hand.

Corporal Buckley, another of my section commanders, had been on leave in India, where he had seen the film, *Last of the Mohicans*. When he set about giving his section hair-cuts before the move, there were some hilarious results and the Mohican ridge was much in evidence. He himself was shaved bald as a Gurkha. My 2-inch mortar man, Bullard, had the victory 'V' sign in tufts from ear to ear; and Bill Hughes' section, a hard-bitten crew at the best of times, looked fiercest of all with an assortment of top knots and moustaches.

THREE

Death Valley

In the grey light of dawn, looking suitably war-like, my platoon set out in two clapped-out lorries with African drivers, following the spoor of the Jap southwards.

My orders to set up a traffic control post were to take us over the erstwhile battle grounds of the Shenan pass and beyond into the ill-famed malaria-ridden valley of the Kabaw, through which our own, and eventually another battalion, were to pass on route for a concentration area near the Chindwin River.

The road, if such it could be called, clung to the side of the mountains in a series of loops, and had a switchback quality made even less attractive by the obvious lack of driving skill with which the two Askaris raced each other around the sickening hairpin bends, brakes squealing and gears clattering madly. By mid-day our nerves were almost at breaking-point and we were caked from head to foot in fine powdery dust, which invaded every orifice of our bodies and covered the trees and bushes along the road side, so that they had become as cocoa-red as the track itself.

Abandoned and burnt-out vehicles of every description adorned the jungle-clad slopes of the precipitous gorges and valleys along the way, and we were inordinately glad when the slow grinding climb of our approach to the summit of the pass began, in contrast to the insanity of our earlier progress.

With less than a mile still to go to the top of the pass, I was watching the rear vehicle making very heavy going of the climb, with steam belching from the radiator, when it suddenly ran off the edge of the road and disappeared down a hillside into the jungle. We stopped and made our way back, wondering what horrific sight would confront us. There, fifty feet down the mountain, we found the wreck of the lorry on its side in the underbush. Scattered over a wide area were a half-platoon of cursing, bruised and shaken soldiery, intent on the murder of the African driver. I arrived on the scene just in time to prevent Sergeant Woods from doing the fellow a mischief with his bayonet. Sitting in the roadside dust, his head in his hands, the poor Askari was rocking back and forth, uttering loud and distinctly animal-like moans.

It was some considerable time, occupied with first aid to the injured and the transfer of loads of baggage to the remaining vehicle, before we were on our way again.

Near the summit of the pass the overheated, not to say over-loaded, Chevrolet truck finally gave up altogether and would soon have joined many others over the mountainside had we not been informed by a passing despatch-rider that a Light Aid Detachment, or 'spanner-shop' as we called them, was operating up ahead. If you have ever had the misfortune to assist in pushing a 30-hundredweight lorry up a very steep gradient in a temperature of 90 degrees in the shade, you will appreciate why I dally with the incident. In rustic English, we were almost knackered by the time we reached the LAD. The REME sergeant who then came to our assistance, scratched his head and deliberated for thirty seconds before delivering his diagnosis:

"Somebody's made a fair cow of this – we'll give her a go and try to get you moving in the morning."

From which we gathered that he was a 'Fair dinkum' Australian mechanic from way back in the outback and that, if anyone could put us on wheels again, he could.

Thankfully we parked ourselves off to one side of the track and settled down to enjoy bully beef stew and incredibly hard biscuits and tea.

Later we wandered onto the ridge from which we witnessed an unforgettable sunset. All around lay the fantastic, cut-off, vast world of harsh, uncharitable peaks and hellish ravines and valleys, with ourselves insignificant ants on the crazy ribbon of red dust which was a vast army's only line of communication.

Dead and still and endless the carpet of green stretched out under the brassy sky. Against the descending sun the battlements were dark and clean-lined, while to the east, where the light poured slantwise, the strange landscape shouted with colour; we were trapped, caught in colour and dazzled by the clarity of the light and the magnificence of its variations. Closer around us the shaved hilltops, flattened trees and twisted stumps, rising from the pockmarked earth, bore silent witness to the fierce battles which had been fought for the ridges commanding the pass. Sergeant Woods and the others who had fought there pointed out the landmarks.

"That's Nippon Hill over there; this here is Scraggy; there's Malta."

The newer men prompted them to tell of their experiences, but they remained strangely reticent. Sergeant Florence summed up the veteran infanteers' feelings:

"You can't describe it, boyo, but I will tell you one thing, look you, it's not like the flamin' pictures, by damn!"

Woods shut them up finally.

"Aw reet then: fall in fer thi mepachrine pills – yer'll find out all yer ever wants ter know int fust five minutes, when tha gets down yon; cumm on then, get thisel fell in."

This was the time of the day I hated most, because of the necessity of taking those unforgettably nasty anti-malaria tablets, which turned our skins a jaundiced yellow. Some said they made men impotent. There was an army order making it obligatory for officers to supervise the taking of the daily dose by their men, and a unit's efficiency was partly judged by the percentage of malaria incidence within its ranks. Undoubtedly the scourge of malaria fever in the past has accounted for more deaths than any war in history.

After that we sat around smoking disgusting Victory V cigarettes, while the men talked idly amongst themselves about home and the coming fighting. I looked again beyond the smashed battlefields and etched the scene once more in my brain, south, west and north. The evening air at that altitude cut into my lungs with dry frost; from a nearby fire the perfumed smell of wood smoke was in my nostrils. I gave a groan of pure ecstatic delight, as though viewing the world from the throne of the gods, and I listened to the men and thought how every safe generality I had gathered so far on my travels seemed always to be cancelled by another. If this moment could have been the whole of war, then I could see the glory in it.

Several thousand feet up, in the tropic night under stars which hung like lanterns in the sky, we slept.

In the golden swirling mists of dawn we piled into our protesting lorry and drove off the ridge as if in a state of flight, hurrying to get away from the unearthly landscape.

The late afternoon changed everything in Death Valley. This grisly nick name for the Kabaw valley had been earned because the deadly scrub typhus, which infected the place, had killed hundreds of fleeing refugees and soldiers in 1942.

The road surface tore viciously at the truck's almost bald tyres and the overloaded springs groaned and squealed in anguish. At last we stopped beside the track in choking dust, amidst the dense teak trees and clumps of bamboo, where we set up the traffic control post. We remained there for almost three weeks.

Japanese graves, marked with wooden uprights inscribed with coloured hieroglyphics, were much in evidence in the valley. Burnt-out enemy trucks, some with the charred remains of their drivers still at the wheel, littered the tracks and dry river beds . . . Near our bivouac area was what remained of a Jap field hospital – nothing but a huddle of leaf-boughed shelters under which lay some four hundred skeletons. The ragged khaki cotton uniforms of the dead flapped languidly in the faint breeze and bloodstained paper bandages lay unravelled in festoons across the branch-woven beds.

The sickening smell of death hovered in the still moist air and pervaded everything. It would have been a gruesome enough experience to spend even three hours in such a place, let alone three weeks. Transport of the 2nd British Division moving forward began to appear in regular convoys, throwing up the evil smelling dust which took hours to settle. Water was rationed to one pint per day for all purposes, so it goes without saying that we never washed, though I did insist on the men shaving in the tea dregs. A great morale booster this, and strangely not difficult to enforce even under such conditions.

Finally our orders came to pack up and occupy another post further forward in the gorge of the Myntha river. Here we swam, when duties permitted, and rid our clothes and bodies of the sickly smell of the Kabaw.

All units forward of Imphal were now being solely supplied from the air. One day when returning from a dropping zone with some rations, Florence and I found an abandoned jeep with the tank full of petrol and a wonky steering wheel. For some time after this I 'swanned' up and down the line of communication, visiting other platoon control posts, which had by now been sent forward from Battalion. But the joy-riding did not last long. Came the day when the Battalion rolled itself up on us, gathering outlying platoons on the way. Colonel Harvey just happened to catch me returning to my post in the jeep.

"I want that toy of yours, young fellow. Bring it forward when you join up with us", he said, "and hand it over to the Mule Transport Officer."

"Yes sir", I said, and touched my forehead dutifully. Jeeping was infinitely better than marching any day, and my Sergeants and I put our scheming heads together to try and find a way to hold on to our newly acquired private transport.

A few miles on at a place called Kalewa, the East African Division ahead of us had secured the Chindwin river crossing after some bitter fighting: the small town was in ruins. The sappers had just completed a gigantic Bailey bridge, which spanned the river beyond the town. We were told it was the longest bridge of its kind ever built, and when I first saw it I was astounded: it seemed to stretch out across that mighty tropical river to infinity.

On the side nearest my control post the engineers had built a ramp down the steep river bank to the bridge. I was travelling up this ramp in my jeep one day, with Smith my batman at the wheel. We had been collecting rations from the Battalion, which at this time was busy doing nothing in a concentration area on the far side of the river. Suddenly the jeep engine stalled; Smith tried holding her with the brakes, but to no effect; we began to run slowly backwards down the ramp and ended up in the water with the jeep almost on top of us. Quickly it sank to the bottom. Scrambling out of the water I thought we had better go back and explain to the MTO. Suddenly there was a warning shout from the air sentries on top of the bank:

"Zeros, Zeros, take cover!"

Smith and I scrambled up the ramp for the nearest slit trench, from which we watched the ensuing dive-bomb attacks.

One after another the Jap planes thundered down, machine guns rattling in awful metallic fury. Several bombs obviously intended for the bridge fell harmlessly with loud whooshing sounds into the river.

Spouting columns of water rose high in the air, level with where we crouched in the trench. I was shaking like a leaf; but Smith seemed to enjoy the spectacle and kept popping his head up and shouting—

"Look at this one boss. Chrrrist! that was near the bridge – watch out, there's another sod coming straight up river."

In due course we ventured back across the bridge. The whole battalion was there. The total casualties for the attack: one mule killed and one jeep lost.

The CO cursed. The MTO cursed. But looking back on my mental anguish when I had watched the jeep sink into the river, I was not at all displeased with the final outcome of the incident. The Jap raid had given me a cast-iron alibi. The MTO was still kicking up a bit of a fuss about the jeep when we took our leave of him. It was with savage delight that I reminded him:

"It was the flaming Japs' fault, not mine – anyway, the brakes didn't bloody work."

Soon afterwards we were shipped downstream on rafts to a forward concentration area at Siswa. Two days later we moved under arms, stripped down to the barest necessities for survival, into the place of honour in the divisional order of march, popularly referred to as "the bleedin' sharp end". For several weeks the march led us inexorably south. Sometimes a distance of fifteen or twenty miles would be covered between 4 am and the early afternoon. The routine remained the same day after monotonous day: march, dig, patrol, stand-to, pack up, move on. A long tortuous file of sweating men and mules, covered in billowing clouds of scented red dust, threaded its way through the trackless forests. After a week or two of this we began to feel that we were alone in the world. Save once on patrol when we were welcomed into a large village in which Burmese refugees from miles around were congregated. We were entertained by the head man, who provided the patrol with some excellent cigars, potent native gin, bananas and a fine repast of nuts, dahl and several more delicacies. I was somewhat embarrassed at having to search the village after such an obviously friendly reception, but my Burmese corporal interpreter insisted that the headman, though benevolent-looking enough, may well have been as amiably disposed to the enemy as he appeared to be to us. Imagine my chagrin when I discovered an antiquated Singer sewing machine in one of the villagers' huts. Up to that point I had fondly assumed we were the first white men ever to set foot in this lost world.

Some days after this incident we emerged at long last from the mountainous jungle country into the dry zone proper. Here in the flat scrub and giant teak forests we marched down endless dry river courses known as *chaungs*. Our water was severely rationed and carried in bulk paniers on the mules. Apart from reserve ammunition, also humped by these patient animals, all else was carried on our own backs: weapons, water bottles, spare socks, steel helmets, plimsolls, a piece of towel and soap, a razor per section, half a blanket and mosquito-net each, perhaps a tin of bully beef and some crumbling biscuits, bayonet, knife, maps, compasses, cigarettes, mess-tins and spoon, and little else besides ammunition and grenades. Some men carried giant tobacco leaves fastened to their packs to dry in the sun, and became adept at rolling cigarettes from these, using pages torn from issue Bibles for papers.

Sometimes we dug in the sand of the chaungs and opened up mud holes from which to replenish our supplies of water and sponge the muzzles of the mules. Always the eternal life-giving tea was priority number one; each section carried a blackened 7-pound jam tin for the purpose, in which was kept the evil-smelling mosquito-netting bag of damp tea leaves.

When we marched by night down the unchanging dusty chaungs, the sand, thick, soft and silent, appeared silvery like snow between the black forest walls in the moon-pale tropical darkness.

Since leaving Kalewa each brigade group had been independently supplied by air with all food, ammunition and mail. The hastily organised dropping zones were many miles apart and we marched for our food.

The objective of the 20th Indian Division was the capture of Monewa, a large town on the Chindwin river near its confluence with the Irrawaddy.

Two companies of my Battalion formed part of a special Force to spearhead the advance: this force was named 'Rushcol', and the Brigade Group had been denuded of its jeeps and 15-hundredweight trucks to put it on wheels. Forced-marching fifty miles, 'Rushcol' encountered strong enemy opposition at a place named Budalin, where (apart from some previous and minor patrol clashes) my company was blooded for the first time in this second campaign.

There was some sniping from hidden Japs as the column approached the town. A platoon of 'C' Company went forward and dealt with the hindrance with only light casualties to themselves. The CO, Lieutenant-Colonel Harvey, then made hurried plans and attacked with the whole column to clear the rest of the town. By nightfall Budalin was in our hands.

There we waited for the remainder of the Brigade Group to join up with us. When they arrived, we were ordered to push on to the Irrawaddy River with all speed. The other two brigades in the Division, the 32nd and 80th, were left to deal with the enemy stronghold at Monywa, which they captured five days later.

On top of an escarpment one evening, we gained our first view of the Irrawaddy river away to the south. As we began to dig ourselves in for the night, the first enemy artillery barrage for many weeks burst in upon us.

The 4th/10th Gurkhas, of our Brigade, went ahead and cleared the large town of Myinmu on the north bank of the Irrawaddy, about forty miles west of Mandalay. Our Divisional Commander, General Gracey, gave orders to search for suitable crossing-places over the river. Approximately a fortnight would be needed to build up in the corps area the supplies and stores that would be required for the coming battle.

It was here that the Japanese turned once again to fight in earnest.

FOUR

The Sharp End

We relieved the 4th/10th Gurkhas in the town of Myinmu and began the job of improving the defences. That night I received orders to stand by for a patrol; the hours of darkness afforded us little, if any, sleep. Just as the light was fading in the western sky, the enemy began to shell our positions with 105-mm guns from emplacements beyond the south bank of the Irrawaddy. I had a lump of bully beef half way to my mouth when I first heard the distant boom-boom. I dived, map of the area in one hand and bully beef in the other, for the nearest trench. Sergeant Woods was as quick, and Smith a shade slower. The shells whistled with a sudden rising shriek and burst ten feet away, one behind and one in front of the trench. The three of us lay, threshing madly like netted fish, at the bottom of the sandy hole, laughing and cursing each other as we struggled to disentangle our limbs.

It was around ten o'clock that my first stint on watch came to an end. I was completing my final round of the company positions, when a party of enemy came close up to our trenches and fired off some light mortar bombs and hurled hand grenades into the mule lines. The sentries kept their own grenades at hand and the Battalion stood-to in the trenches ready to receive an attack; but none came. There were rows of old ration tins hanging on trip wires about 30 or 40 yards from the lines, to give us warning of approaching enemy. Occasionally these tins clattered, but the Japs never came into view and the rest of the night passed uneventfully. At dawn one of my sections made a patrol of the perimeter of our trenches to a depth of 300 yards around the Battalion area, only to find a few heaps of expended cartridge cases here and there, together with some gently cooling piles of excreta, where the enemy 'jitter' party had relieved themselves before clearing off. I thought, how like the reflex action so often noted by policemen investigating burglaries, when the crooks leave their filth on the carpet.

At mid-day I visited the Battalion command post in the middle of the village, where John Dyer, the Intelligence Officer, gave me the details of my patrol. My orders were to establish an observation post somewhere between the villages of Wetto and Satpangon, which were some seven or eight miles down river. My task was to report all movements on the enemy side of the Irrawaddy. Apparently the area had been chosen tentatively as the most likely starting-point for our divisional river-crossing: air photographs showed firm ground leading down to the water's edge and plenty of cover to hide the troops and equipment as they formed up. Intelligence also had it that there were no Japanese permanently posted opposite my proposed patrol base and it was thought to face the boundary between two enemy divisions.

The information of most interest to me, at the time, was that I was being ordered to a place on the safer side of a mile-wide water obstacle where, although it was by no means certain that all the enemy had departed, my men and I might well find time to relax and enjoy the scenery. It was with a certain relief that I viewed the situation and relished the prospect of getting away from the main body of the Battalion for a while. Now and then my salvation seemed infinitely more secure in my own hands.

Sergeant Florence reported the platoon ready with full complement of ammunition and five days' 'K' rations per man. The sun was sinking rapidly, and all was quiet in the Battalion trenches as the men stood to. It seemed that we must have been doing this at dusk and dawn all our lives, so much a part of our daily routine had it become.

An hour later, with the sun gone and the mosquitoes buzzing, the enemy's 105-mm guns again opened their evening hate in our direction; shells tore through the air close above the heads of the Battalion with the roar of an express train, and burst behind the village with a rumble like rocks tumbling down a gully.

The telephone in my command post buzzed and Sergeant Woods answered it. Turning to me he said:

"Mr Gordon is coming across with the Assault Pioneer Platoon, Sir. As soon as he takes over our positions, we're to move out."

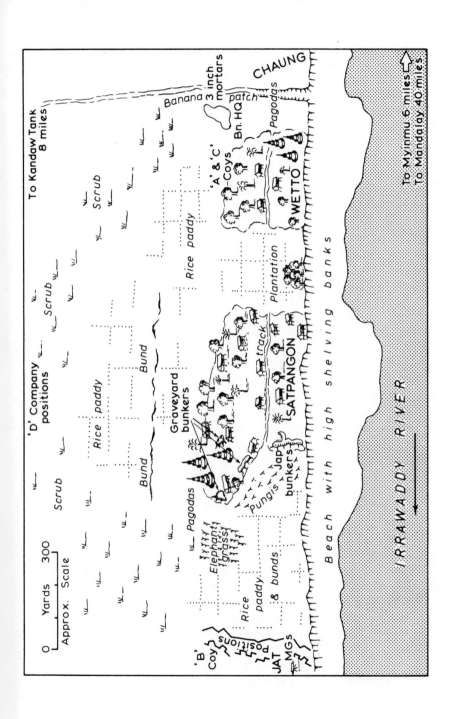

The route I had planned was to take us on a north-westerly course for six miles, when I expected we should be near enough due north of the eastern end of the village of Wetto. My idea was to approach our final objective, having first ensured that Wetto itself was clear of enemy, rather than march at the point selected as the patrol base, not knowing what was on at least one flank when we got there.

During the march, a curious tension was building up inside me, and a dark sense of foreboding filled my thoughts. It was a warning I had experienced too often to ignore, and I was pleased that Woods, out in front with the compass, seemed to be moving with every animal sense alert.

Although the main Jap force was supposed to be clear of this north bank of the river and engaged in preparing and planning its new defence line on the other side, I was none too confident that this was entirely correct. It occured to me that the enemy 'jitter patrol' of the previous night would hardly have remained in the area so long, unless they had some operating base on this side of the river.

We were all rather edgy, sweaty and tense with the weight of our equipment, the inevitable halts to check the compass bearings, and the messages whispered up and down the column to maintain distance. At last, after about three hours marching through the soft sand and thorny scrub, the word came back from Sergeant Woods that his scouts were entering a dry watercourse, which appeared to run straight down to the river. Checking my map under Smith's half blanket to shield the light of my torch, I found that the stream-bed traced the eastern edge of the village of Wetto and should give us excellent cover and an ideal approach. I decided to take over the lead of the column myself in order to select a point lower down the chaung from which to plan the next step. About half an hour later we were moving in short bounds, covered by scouts on each flank on the high banks of the stream-bed, while the remainder of the platoon in single file moved silently in the soft sand below. Then I caught a brief, but distinct whiff of fish, and thought I heard the lapping of water. Thompson, from the leading section, who had been scouting ahead a few yards, slithered down the chaung to me and reported that we were not far from the Irrawaddy.

Near the river bank and the tiny dry delta formed by the stream-bed, we discovered four or five upturned Burmese country boats, and beyond the bank of the chaung on our right we could make out the outline of a large village, about a hundred and fifty yards away.

The Section Commanders gave whispered orders to the men to take up positions of all-round defence, whilst I crawled up the bank to reconnoitre. I could make out two pagodas with their tall 'umbrellas' standing out starkly amongst some palm trees, and below them the roofs of a few stilted bamboo buildings partially hidden by the trees and undergrowth surrounding the village. Woods and Florence crawled up and lay breathing heavily on either side of me. Twenty yards away on our left, the Irrawaddy, awesome in its immensity, flowed silently by on its way to the sea.

The night was quiet. There was not enough breeze to tinkle the pagoda bells. In Wetto nothing stirred. We lay straining for the slightest sound, the sweat cooling on us, for perhaps twenty minutes. Presently I began to shiver slightly.

"What time do you reckon on getting to the patrol base, sir?" Sergeant Woods had rolled closer and whispered in my ear.

I could sense his impatience and felt annoyed by it. Motioning both Sergeants to follow, I returned to the bottom of the chaung.

"I don't like the look of this place and my bloody hair keeps standing on end." Florence sniggered as I finished speaking.

Both he and Woods were obviously feeling bored and I wondered, fine soldiers though they were, if perhaps they were a little too lacking in imagination at times like these. They obviously thought I was acting over-cautiously. I had decided to reconnoitre further myself before moving the platoon on, more to reassert my authority than anything else, I think. Telling them to remain in the chaung with the platoon, I went off with Smith.

Moving along the sandy beach under cover of the river bank, we began to crawl on our stomachs towards Wetto. Without the burden of equipment and rifles, which we had left in the chaung, I suddenly felt light and free. As we slithered forward, I wondered if the safety-pins on the grenades we carried inside our jungle-green battle-blouses would remain securely in position.

It was darker somehow, nearer the village, and the trees grew within ten or twenty yards of the water's edge. A few yards up the beach were some more country boats, and we made for these. We had barely got behind the first one, when someone cleared his throat nearby. I felt my neck hairs bristle and froze with my face in the sand, every nerve straining and tense. A voice, which was definitely not Burmese, spoke as if the owner had his mouth full of water and was answered by another. I raised my eyes and saw, not ten feet away, two Japanese soldiers with canvas-covered helmets on their heads. One of them began to urinate in the sand, the other squatted nearby, his trousers rolled down. Smith's head turned towards me and I could see the white of his eyes. Slowly he brought up his hand and showed me a grenade. I thought at first he would draw the pin and throw the bomb at the Japanese. I moved my head from side to side as rapidly as I dared. I felt him gradually relax.

After what seemed an age there was a grunt and a cough from the Jap nearest us, and then the other, saying something and laughing, walked off towards the darkness of the village. The first one stood up, adjusted his trousers, and kicked some sand over his filth. Some of it landed on my back. Then picking up a long rifle from the ground at his feet, he followed the other Jap into the village.

After about a quarter of an hour we crawled back along the river bank into the chaung where the platoon waited. As Woods and Florence came towards us, I felt a smug sense of superiority.

"What's form, Smudger?" Woods whispered at Smith.

"Same as bleeding usual – Japs shitting all over the place," Smith replied.

FIVE

Pagodas of Wetto

The possibility of my patrol making contact with the enemy on our own side of the Irrawaddy had not really occurred to me very forcibly until now, and I felt betrayed and angry. These odd, wandering enemy would obviously interfere with what I had anticipated as being a few days' laze in the sunshine. . . .

Eventually I decided we would remain where we were in the chaung until first light and then take a further look around after radioing Battalion of what we were up to. Listening posts of three men were placed at either end of the chaung and sentries posted above our positions near the country boats, while the remainder relaxed. Sergeant Woods wanted to drop a couple of 2-inch mortar bombs into Wetto, just to see what would happen. Whether or not his suggestion was made by way of maintaining his reputation of being one of the most aggresive NCOs in the Battalion, I couldn't decide, but I swore at him moodily and received in return one of his "Now, now, don't get upset, son!" looks.

The rest of the night was uneventful and we spent it resting and changing sentries and listening posts. I did not feel particularly tired until dawn, when the eastern sky became a mass of colour and a rustling breeze suddenly made the pagoda bells tinkle, reminding me that the next round of the contest was about to begin.

I was rather ashamed of my irresolute feelings: I imagined the NCOs must be thinking that we should have been poised at the edge of Wetto by then, alert and ready to pounce on whoever lurked there.

"Cover half a section from here. We'll take the rest across, when they've cleared as far as the pagodas."

I thought that would do for a starter, and Woods jumped to it straight away. Corporal Hughes led his rifle group towards the village without comment. The rest of us lay tensely waiting along the bank of the chaung.

There was a wispy ground mist and the trees, the pagodas, and the basha roofs seemed to be suspended above it eerily like some ghostly water colour.

Slowly Bill Hughes and his men stalked towards the village and then disappeared into the mist. After a minute or two one of the men re-emerged and signalled us to advance. Joining the rifle group hurriedly, we found ourselves in a well-maintained vegetable patch enclosed by a post-and-rail fence. From the bottom of this ran a wide dusty track which was the main street of Wetto, running straight between thatched and stilted wooden huts, each with its own plot of enclosed garden.

To the left of the track, between it and the river, were three pink and white gold-leafed pagodas, about thirty feet high, standing together on a tiled patio surrounded by a low plaster wall. The dawn breeze had dropped suddenly and there was a deathly quiet. Wetto was a ghost village, seemingly deserted but somehow menacing.

In extended order, using the main track as an axis, we advanced cautiously, the men searching each hut and scanning the trees and bushes with practised skill. Beneath some of the bashas were deep pits – dug-outs which were obviously intended as air-raid shelters for the villagers.

There was something ominous in the stillness and emptiness of the place. But then many of these villages had been evacuated by the Burmese to escape the fighting, and it was not unusual for the people to band together in one of the larger, more inaccessible townships, until it was safe to return to their own homes. But in Wetto the huts were still furnished and there were cooking utensils, some of which contained half-cooked rice.

After about a quarter of an hour we came upon a large fenced enclosure in which there were twenty or so scraggy cattle. These beasts began to herd together quite quietly as we approached, until they were bunched on the further side of the corral.

Moving slowly around the enclosure we continued our stealthy advance, until quite suddenly the trees and huts ended abruptly. Beyond we could see the gently rising paddyfields across which, at a distance of probably 300 yards, was the beginning of another village. Halfway between, near the river bank, stood a group of trees and bushes forming a small plantation about twenty yards· square.

Remaining in cover and taking up firing positions, we gazed across at the plantation and the village looming beyond with its tall wispy palms.

The small plantation seemed an ideal hiding-place for our observation post; it looked as if it would be shady and cool in the heat of the day. It was high enough above the river to give a view both up and downstream for several miles, and an approach could be made to it without exposing ourselves to the watchful eyes of the enemy posts, should there be any on the other bank of the Irrawaddy.

The large village beyond the plantation was Satpangon. After conferring with Woods and Florence, I decided to have a closer look at the plantation and post the first observation patrol there, before moving the rest of the platoon back to the chaung in which we had spent the night. The chaung, being situated in open scrub, would give us a good field of view in all directions and our radio would not be screened by trees. Since the observation post would be withdrawn at night anyway, we had to decide on a firm base which could be adequately defended. The prospect of using Wetto itself, tempting though it was, we agreed was out of the question owing to its size.

The sun was beginning to warm us and with it our spirits rose. Smith and I stepped out onto the paddy to recce the small plantation, whilst Sergeant Woods prepared the first group for OP duty. As we left the sheltering village and began to walk forward, my nostrils were suddenly assailed by the familiar sweet, sickly smell of decomposing flesh. Smith pointed to something half concealed in the short, brown grass and I hurried towards him. My palms began to sweat and the tension returned as I saw lying before me the remains of an Indian soldier. His boots were missing; his face was covered by a mass of flies and maggots. One leg was contorted under the body like the limb of a rag doll. Smith knelt and examined the divisional sign on the man's sleeve – a black circle of cloth enclosing a silver kukri. The man was from our own Division.

No one had told us that other patrols had visited the area, and yet here was evidence that Pathans from our Division had been there, and, from the look of the corpse we had found, within the last three days.

Something drew us on, although some sixth sense made me acutely aware of hidden eyes watching every movement we made. I found myself on the point of bolting for cover in the village where my platoon was waiting. Smith walked on apparently unconcerned. I followed him, nerves taut and strained and my gaze darting in every direction at once. When we reached the comparative safety of the plantation, I found myself in a bath of perspiration and it was as much as I could do to remain outwardly calm. We had been assailed by enough mystery already, but there in the middle of the copse, stacked neatly as though ready for loading into transport, were twenty or thirty packed haversacks of Indian pattern. Was it just possible, I asked myself, that a patrol of ours had gone over the river from here already?

At that moment I needed the comforting council of my old sweats, and the sooner the better. I could not rid myself of a sickening, almost animal urge to hide myself, and nothing seemed to add up correctly. For some reason I was very jittery and temporarily incapable of making any decision. Certainly, however, I was not prepared to leave any of my men in the copse until I had had time to think about the events of the morning so far. The looming threat of the village of Satpangon had made us all feel uneasy and apprehensive, and the smell of death seemed to stick in our nostrils. It was an uncanny awareness, some kind of sixth sense, which held us as Smith and I rejoined the platoon.

I explained my anxiety as best I could to the NCOs, who seemed no less perplexed when I told them what Smith and I had found. Not even Woods seemed prepared to venture across the intervening ground to Satpangon. Eventually I decided to withdraw to the chaung and wireless the Battalion with our report which by then was an hour overdue.

We left Wetto via the north-east corner of the village, so as to remain hidden whilst crossing the scrub to our chaung. About half way there we entered a small banana grove, the eastern end of which was less than thirty yards from the dry river-bed. This was the first time we had noticed the banana patch and I immediately decided that its size and shade was admirably suited to our needs as a temporary resting-place, perhaps even as the eventual patrol-base, as soon as things had sorted themselves out a little more.

It was about 7.30 am. As we had not eaten for more than twelve hours, we set about preparing breakfast of biscuits and bully beef and tea.

Two men went off down the chaung with the water bottles to replenish our supply for the day, while the mist over the Irrawaddy still gave us cover from possible prying eyes across the water.

I sat down, my back against the trunk of a banana tree, and began to smoke. Some of the men cut down green bananas and began testing their flavour delightedly. Obviously the soldiers' maxim, "when in doubt, brew up," was having its effect so far as they were concerned. Their optimism and the general slackening of tension transmitted itself to me, so that I began to think more clearly about our position.

The signaller was busy getting his radio set working, when Smith came to me carrying a stained mug of steaming tea.

"Here you are, sir; Sergeant Major's brew. Just what the doctor ordered."

As I began to sip gratefully at the sweet syrupy fluid, two shots rang out – crack-thump, crack-thump. The mug fell to the ground as I began to run crouching towards the edge of the banana patch. I saw the two men on water fatigue disappearing in a welter of water bottles, rifles and red dust down the bank of the chaung. Thompson, on sentry duty nearby, lay on his stomach aiming his rifle at a point near the base of the Wetto pagodas. He fired a couple of snap shots and reloaded. Then he told me that the men on water fatigue had come up the chaung, until they were about thirty yards away, and had been fired on when they had climbed the bank. Thompson had seen puffs of smoke from the edge of the village near the pagodas.

The two men crawled in with the water, looking a bit sheepish. One of them, Pile, had a neat hole through the crown of his bush hat and the heel shot away from one of his boots.

Suddenly we heard wailing and shrieking from the direction of the village, and then a horde of Burmese, mostly men and children, about a hundred in all, burst out of Wetto and ran towards us. They were obviously panic-stricken. We could scarcely believe our eyes.

As the natives in the lead reached the banana patch in which we were lying, they caught sight of us and veered away, still running and more terrified than ever. One of the stragglers, a youngish man who seemed more in control of himself, kept turning back the way he had come, brandishing his arms and shouting something unintelligible, either to the other natives or to someone in the village.

Woods ran out a yard or two to head the chap off, which immediately brought a burst of light-machine-gun fire from the direction of the pagodas. Unperturbed, he grabbed the native, hauled him across his shoulders and ran stumbling towards us. The Burmese kicked and screamed, trying to escape, and we had to hold him in the shelter of the trees where Woods had dumped the poor fellow down at my feet.

I now realised, in retrospect, that we must have been constantly under observation since Smith and I had found the packs in the plantation outside Satpangon, or possibly even before that. Either the villagers had been well concealed in some obscure shelters, when we were searching Wetto, or, as we had withdrawn from there, they had been herded after us by the Japanese. At any rate I was at last convinced that Satpangon was well and truly occupied by the enemy. I guessed that when the Japs had taken pot-shots at my water carriers, the Burmese had broken from the village to escape what was all too obviously about to become a battlefield.

I addressed the native, who was still grovelling in the dust at my feet, whilst a few shots were exchanged between the Japanese and my men from the edge of the banana patch. He could not understand my few words of Burmese. I tried Urdu, which seemed to bring some response, but he answered so rapidly that I had difficulty in following. Slowly I tried again, and finally got the following story:

"I am headman of Wetto village. About a month ago, many Japani wallah came over river to village . . ."

"How many?" I asked.

"About a thousand – the people were all made to work, digging trenches and cutting down trees to place over them in Satpangon. Four days ago Indian soldiers came to river with boats. The Japani killed them all and threw their bodies into the Irrawaddy. Now the Japani have taken all young women into Satpangon and my wife is with them."

The headman's story added up, except with regard to the numbers of Japanese involved. There could be thirty or forty, perhaps even three or four hundred within spitting distance of us, but I doubted it very much. Either way our standing patrol mission was 'off' and something else was 'on'. Whatever that turned out to be would depend on how my CO viewed the situation.

I ordered Miller, the signaller, to open up on the Battalion wireless net and prepare to send a message. . . .

"Enemy force, strength unknown, vicinity Satpangon, contact made 07.35 hours. Proceeding to occupy Wetto. No casualties."

Leaving the signaller to encode the message, I went over to the edge of the banana patch, where the firing had stopped and the men were busily packing rations and tea cans and preparing to move.

I sent Corporal Butterworth with his section, covered by the remainder of the platoon, towards the pagodas. They took their time about it, but eventually a runner came back and gave us the all-clear. Once more we entered Wetto near the pagodas, where Butterworth had found several piles of empty cartridge cases, but no other signs of the enemy.

Opening out into extended line again, we began to repeat the searching operation of earlier that morning, but this time more throughly. Two of the lads went into a basha where they found a couple of trussed fowls hanging from the ceiling. As one of them tried to pull the chickens down there was a flash and explosive crack, as a hidden booby-trap went off, almost bringing the hut down on their heads. They came out coughing and spluttering, but unhurt, with dust in their eyes and ears. At once we heard the dull thud-thud of mortars being fired from the direction of Satpangon. We were close to the corral of native cattle as the first salvo of bombs straddled it, bursting in the branches of the trees on either side. The air was thick with red-hot swishing metal and clouds of dust, as more bombs burst all around us and amongst the panic-stricken animals, which began to stampede in all directions. The noise was deafening, and only the presence of the Burmese air-raid shelters saved us from ignoble retreat and many casualties. The mortaring went on for some time, ranging up and down the village. I was scared stiff of the enemy following this up with a direct assault. We were in deep shelters from which we had no field of fire, and the men had split up all over the place when they had taken refuge from the bombing. If the Burmese headman's estimate of the Jap strength was only half correct, we would be in a sorry plight if they attacked us.

It was about 9 am. I hoped that Battalion had received my message and would let us know before much longer how they wanted us to get on with the war.

After what seemed an age, the mortaring stopped and there was no argument when I gave the order to withdraw from Wetto once again. Miller looked rather anxious when we reached him in the banana patch. He and Bullard and Morrisroe had been left there alone with the radio, when we had followed Butterworth into the village. The intensity of the mortar bombardment had made them imagine all kinds of awful fates for the platoon.

There was a message from Battalion ordering me to remain where I was and await reinforcements.

Providing the Japanese allowed us the option, we could sit it out in the banana patch and take a breather.

SIX

Aunt Sallies

Fifteen hours had elapsed since we had left the main body of the Battalion. Mundane as events had been, we were nevertheless tense and tired, and any excuse to leave the war to someone else for a while was very welcome.

I posted sentries and Bren guns in company with Sergeant Woods and checked over the platoon. So far no casualties . . . apart from Pile's hat and boot. The poor Burman, who had remained with the signallers and platoon HQ during the mortaring period, was obviously a very frightened man. Eventually Smith persuaded him to smoke a cigarette. Sitting on his heels, he held the cigarette between the third and fourth fingers of his right hand and drew the smoke through the clasped palm. I was thankful, as previously his moans and wailing had been getting on my nerves and I was sure he could be heard by every Jap for miles around.

Woods and Florence were discussing how many cattle had been killed by the bombing. They hoped that the Battalion would come up and occupy Wetto, so that we could get at the fresh meat before it went off. I could sympathise with this: most of us had not eaten anything fresh, let alone meat, for well over a year. For three hours there was not a sound to be heard but the whispering of a faint breeze amongst the banana leaves, and now and then the tinkling of the pagoda bells in Wetto.

About mid-day the sentries saw a column about a mile off moving towards us from the north-east through the scrub and haze. It was Major Kitley with 'D' Company, less one platoon – about sixty or seventy men all told, with Charlie Bates as the only other Company officer. I wondered vaguely why my own Company had not been sent.

The Major had recently arrived as a reinforcement from

England, where he had been an instructor at a Battle School. My only acquaintance with him before this had been during a recent march when, at the night halt, he had taken a short religious service for some of the more devout men. I could see the bulge of his issue Bible, in the left breast pocket of his battle blouse, as he came and sat beside me.

Charles, his large blonde moustache drooping with sweat from the forced march, dropped down beside us in the dust under the banana trees, which I had by now come to regard as our temporary home.

I gave my report to Kitley and told him what I had gleaned from the Burman. Kit thought my estimate of the Japanese strength too high, despite the amount of mortar fire, and seemed determined to have a shot at clearing Satpangon immediately. I wanted him to occupy Wetto properly first and probe around for a bit; but he said he had been ordered to clear Satpangon before last light, and that my platoon was to come under his command. Charles looked non-committal. After a while we set off once again towards Wetto, which Kit had agreed was the best way to approach the Jap positions. Even as a hundred or so of us moved off, I cannot say that I felt at all confident of the outcome of the operation. I remembered the mortaring, and with that amount of armament at its disposal, the Jap force surely must be more than a wandering band awaiting its chance to cross over the river.

Kitley had decided that he needed his right flank well out in the scrub, whilst the main body went through Wetto. He gave this job to two of my sections. I left the third section, with my sergeants and platoon HQ, back in the banana grove to relay wireless reports to Battalion.

The sun was high overhead and the heat and dust settled like a shroud on my normally high spirits. As we kept abreast of the main body, I could catch glimpses from time to time of Kitley's tall figure moving hither and thither between his sections and platoons, as they advanced between the trees and stilted bamboo huts. I remember smiling to myself at the way Kitley was conducting the 'show', and I heard Bullard remark to the man next to him something about "a bloody battle exercise".

"Any minute that geezer will call us all in a circle and give us the bleedin' school solution!"

Actually everything was according to the book and going very nicely so far, but in another 200 yards we would have been going up the rice paddyfields into Satpangon as if we were on Salisbury Plain. . . . Then out of the northern sky came a tiny Auster aeroplane. I thought: "how cool and detached it looks". The spotter aircraft climbed over Satpangon; then, making a climbing turn over the river, it clattered down towards us, waggling its wings. The pilot's head was distinct. He put out a hand and waved. Something fell towards us, fluttering on the lines of a miniature parachute. Weighted coloured streamers arranged themselves on a nearby bush. The plane zoomed, banked and turned away, with the men swearing and waving towards it:

"Lucky swine! Wish I were up there with that."

"Yer wouldn't like to be up there without it."

I reached the message first and read:

Approx. 300 Nips NW corner SATPANGON stop Corner with pagodas stop Good luck stop Signed Duck, the man who could — like a rabbit.

"Some sense of humour," I thought. "Anyway, that information will give Kitley something to think about."

The troops all around had gone to ground and I moved across to where the Major was standing, not twenty yards from the edge of Wetto. He was obviously flushed with the apparent success of the sweep so far, and he waved to Charles and me as we moved through the scrub towards him. As we approached I heard him say to his CSM, who was kneeling behind a tree:

"What a terrible smell there is here, Sar'n't Major!" I told him about the dead Indian out in the paddyfield. For some reason Kitley wanted to see the body, but then changed his mind. Perhaps he was beginning to realise that there really were men not far away who were fully intent on doing to us what they had done to the Indian.

Charles said he thought we should not cross the paddy without support, and that, with the scrub and the broken ground to the north, we might get close enough to have a real scout before committing ourselves. I think Kit was glad of Charles' counsel and made a plan on the lines he had suggested. In five minutes we were off again.

The company was strung out loosely, with a point section and scouts out in front. As we moved along the blind side of a high bund parallel to Satpangon, Kitley dropped off Bren guns to give us their covering fire should it be needed.

There was no movement in Satpangon and the thick undergrowth which surrounded it obscured the huts and pagodas from our view, although we were no more than 150 to 200 yards away from it.

Crossing occasional gaps in the high bund, which was surmounted with a thorn hedge, did not draw fire onto us and Kitley undoubtedly became impatient. He ordered the main body to line the bund, and then sent Corporal Andrews with the point section through the thin scrub, whilst the remainder of us covered them. As I watched Andrews move off with his section, I suddenly thought of fairground Aunt Sallies and wanted to call out to them: "Come back. Come back." A machine-gun clattered, piercing the silence like a needle through a blanket. Andrews knelt down slowly, then rolled forward on his face. The man next to him – and the regulation five paces distant – spun round like a top and flopped in a heap beside Andrews. Two other men – the Bren gun team – dropped into a fold in the ground and fired one burst, before the traversing Jap gun found them.

Along the bund, men were sliding quietly backwards, faces in the gravel. At least three more machine-guns and many rifles were being fired from the Japanese positions, and sending hot lead hurtling into the bund and into the head of anyone crazy enough to raise himself into a firing position.

Amid this uproar which tore at the brain came back the only survivor of the point section, the Aunt Sallies – Private Webb, a swarthy Liverpool Irishman, tattooed from waist to neck, his right arm hanging in shreds and his face pale green with shock and fear.

"Jesus! Mary, Mother o' God! Andy's dead. I couldn't get him back. Did the others make it?"

Webb's face was lacerated by the thorns where he had burst through the hedge on top of the bund. A stretcher-bearer slipped down beside him and began to cut away Webb's sleeve . . . and with it the strips of flesh which had been holding the arm to his shoulder.

The shooting continued. From our point of view the target presented was merely the edge of the village; whereas if one stayed in a firing position on the bund for more than a few seconds at a time, it brought down fairly accurate rifle fire from the Japanese. Many of them must have been concealed in sniping-posts high up in the trees. Several of the men near me were lying with their shirts and faces covered in blood, and their mates were doing their best to render some sort of first aid with their field dressings.

Lawson and Bullard crawled up, lugging the 2 inch mortar. They began to fire over the bund at a fairly low angle, so that the bombs burst among the trees. Some of the smoke bombs had an incendiary effect, and eventually they succeeded in starting several fires in the village. This helped to thicken up the smoke-screen. I saw that Charles had begun to move some of the men back from the bund through the scrub towards what appeared to be broken ground in the rear. They went in groups of two and three, helping the wounded and lugging what looked like a lifeless body by the pack-straps.

A few feet away, protruding through the thorn hedge on the bund, was a discarded Bren gun. The Japs were firing indiscriminately at us now through the smoke. I thought I saw movement in the branches of one of the higher trees. Squirming behind the Bren and peering carefully through the thorn hedge, I suddenly saw high up the unmistakable flash of an automatic weapon. Taking aim, I loosed off practically a full magazine into the tree and was rather surprised to see something thresh down out of the branches and begin to swing like a pendulum above the roof of a burning hut.

"You got the sod, sir. He's on the end of a bloody rope." Smith was jubilant as he leaned across to slap another magazine down beside the gun.

As I glanced at Smith, I saw Kitley's tall figure striding towards us quite upright, head and shoulders in full view of the enemy.

"Who the hell gave you the order to pull back?" he roared at me. Obviously he was very angry and beside himself with the shambles his company appeared to be in. Smith looked up and shouted at him:

"Get your head down, sir, for Christ's sake!"

As he spoke, I saw the Major sinking slowly to the ground, his face ashen grey and his mouth agape. A bullet from one of the keen-eyed Jap tree-snipers had gone through Kitley's groin at a deflecting angle downwards, and had come out again low down behind his thigh.

Charles appeared crouching low.

"Come on, Coop, get your skates on. God! Has he bought one?"

Kitley's eyes opened and he said quietly:

"Promise you will try and get Andrews back."

Then he fainted again. Charles plugged the bullet holes using our field dressings, and then said:

"Come on, let's get to hell out of this."

Smith and I threw a couple of smoke grenades over the bund to give us some cover. The three of us dragged and carried the Bren gun and Kitley's dead weight, and staggered blindly towards the bushes a hundred yards away where the others were waiting.

Kit's own CSM and the sergeants had organised a rough defensive area, and the men were making some attempt to dig themselves in. The ground was very hard and their entrenching tools were making little impression. Luckily there were some high bunds and thick scrub around: these afforded some cover and protection from the enemy rifle fire which was still quite heavy. We had now about 300 yards of no-man's-land between ourselves and Satpangon, with some fields of fire for our Bren guns. There were eight or nine wounded with us, and out in front of the bund we could see the bodies of Corporal Andrews and his section. The short dry grass around them was burning and there were more black patches against the thick bushes at the edge of the village.

My third section and part of my platoon headquarters, with my wireless set, were still back, I hoped, at the banana patch, nearly half a mile away. 'D' Company's wireless, I was told, was over near the bund, smashed by a Jap bullet. The operator had wriggled out of the harness to give himself more freedom of movement, whilst helping back his mate, who had been hit in the neck.

Charles wanted me to get the wounded out of the way and get a report back to Battalion. He said he would hold on where he was and try to keep tabs on the Japanese meantime. I agreed to this and promised to move back up to the western end of Wetto after dark, so that we could maintain contact and be near enough to the river to get water.

After what seemed an age, I got my sections and the wounded on the move, and, keeping well back in the scrub, we made our way slowly towards the banana grove. It took us so long that it was almost dark when I sent a couple of men ahead to find Woods and the other men of my platoon. After a while shadowy figures came towards us and, as I stood up, a voice which I had certainly not expected to hear said:

"Ah, there you are, young Coop. What have you been up to since I saw you last?"

Peter Gillam's voice was like music in my ears. He was the Battalion's senior Company Commander, and I gathered he had brought two companies and the 3-inch mortars forward from Myinmu and that they were already digging in furiously in Wetto.

The Regimental Medical Officer had established a temporary aid post near the pagodas. I left 'D' Company's wounded there with him and went to find Woods and Florence and the others of my little band. Apparently they had kept the Battalion wireless net open throughout the afternoon, as they listened to our skirmish with the Japs, and had then guided Peter and the Battalion into position just before last light.

The 3-inch Mortar Platoon was in occupation of our banana patch. It was preparing to range onto Satpangon and the bund in front of the position where I had left Charles and the men of 'D' Company. When I saw Peter again and asked him what to do next, he ordered me to occupy the western edge of Wetto, the end directly opposite the Japs, because I obviously knew the area and the ground better than anyone else.

While I waited for Sergeant Woods to bring the platoon forward, Peter sent off a patrol under Sergeant Finnegan of 'C' Company with orders to set up an OP on the other side of the Japs, about 500 yards beyond the western end of Satpangon. I did not envy Finnegan his task. It meant a march of a mile or more in the dark around behind 'D' Company, and then out into the unknown and probably enemy-infested scrub down to the river. To all intents and purposes this patrol would be cut off from us when daylight came.

By about 9 or 10 pm, my platoon were well dug in with a line of trip wire and booby-traps out in front. The left-flank section was close to the river, and Florence had seen to it that the men's water bottles had been replenished and everything was ship-shape for the night.

At about half-hour intervals, 25-pounder guns began harassing the Jap positions with high-explosive salvos, while we were digging our trenches. The presence of most of the Battalion and the sound of our guns was comforting. I had settled back to smoke under my blanket. Then the Intelligence Officer arrived.

"Just thought I would come over and see how you are, old boy." John Dyer had been a schoolmaster before the war. He'd seen plenty of action as a Platoon Commander, knew the score, and was always friendly and calm.

His opening gambit did not fool me one bit. The IO never came near me unless there was some dirty work afoot. My heart began to hammer.

"Come on, John, what the hell now?"

"Got to keep old Jappo keyed up, me boy," he replied. "Peter wants you to go over and take a look around over there."

He gestured towards the black silhouette of Satpangon rising beyond the paddy.

"Well, you can go over yourself, you old sod. We've done enough for one day . . ."

I allowed the ensuing silence to tell on him before relenting.

"Alright, alright, what's the dope?"

The gunners had been called on to 'stonk' the Japs for five minutes at midnight. After that I was supposed to walk across no-man's-land and try and grab a Jap. I did not think much of the idea and I said so in no uncertain terms.

Bullard and Smith said they would come along; but they did not seem very enthusiastic, to say the least. About an hour later shells came screaming in from the north, and the end of Satpangon facing us became a crashing inferno. The high explosive split and ripped into the trees and huts of the village. The luminous dial of my wristwatch showed five minutes past the hour. The bombardment stopped. I climbed out of the trench, followed by the other two, and a few seconds later stumbled over the body of the dead Indian. The stench was sickening and followed us all the way to the copse where Smith and I had found the packs about eighteen hours previously. I had thought I was afraid then, but by comparison I was now almost petrified and convinced that my number was just about up.

We walked on, weapons and grenades at the ready and our hearts in our mouths. There was a stillness and quiet except for the occasional crackling of small fires inside the village. The night air was sweet with the smell of wood smoke.

If the beggars were all asleep after that shelling, they were either stupid or drugged, I thought. My mind conjured up a picture of the Japs all cosily dossed down in deep dug-outs, snuggling up to the Burmese women the village headman had told me about. A movement nearby, which I sensed rather than saw, registered on my brain. Smith's Sten-gun blasted the silence with a long burst. There was a scream and a threshing in the bushes. Bullard flung a phosphorus grenade underhand and it almost asphyxiated us when it burst. A Jap machine-gun fired from a few yards away. Our nerves broke and we began to run like stags for the safety of our own lines. There were a few shots and the explosion of a grenade behind us. We only sprinted all the harder until we fell sprawling over the parapets of my platoon's trenches. The firing stopped, and I lay shivering under my half blanket at the bottom of the slit trench and said my prayers.

At 3 am Sergeant Woods roused me to take my turn on sentry-watch until Stand-to at 4.30 am.

It was nearly thirty-six hours since we had left Myinmu at the start of our abortive patrol. Our experiences since then had left us very tired, our nerves taut like piano wires, with filthy skins, sweat-soaked clothes, and mouths that were dry and evil-tasting.

As we buckled our equipment for the Stand-to. I began to feel slightly more secure. Having paid one visit to the enemy during the night, I thought it was unlikely that we should be required for any more rough games, for a little while at least.

I had unfortunately not reckoned with Peter Gillam's plans. He was sitting on a log in the dark when the runner took me to him. It occurred to me that here was a man with an opportunity to make a name for himself and the Battalion quickly – and nothing was going to stop him. His tough, rotund figure had the mark 'professional' stamped all over it, and I recalled how he had greeted me when I first joined the Battalion.

"I'm Bligh, welcome aboard the 'Bounty'."

I had learned since that Peter was a colourful, competent and expert fighting soldier. Brought up in the days before the war when the Army liked its eccentrics, the pose suited his seniority and personality admirably.

He pushed his bush-hat to the back of his head and looked up at me with the quizzical grin which I had come to know so well.

"Chrisssst, me boy, you didn't give the Japs much of a party last night, did you?"

I felt somewhat aggrieved at his remark, and unjustly admonished, but I knew the drill well: Never complain, never explain – it's a sign of weakness. Grunting something which might have been "Good morning", I tried to appear unconcerned and at ease. I knew that Peter was weighing something in his mind, and it was not concerning my visit to the Jap positions. He must have known that I was expecting some slight respite and probably said what he had to test my reaction. I suspected that he had been wondering whether he could use me usefully again and soon, whilst still getting some return for his money. Then he said:

"I want you to take your platoon. Get them round to the west of the Japs before first light, dig in and make sure that none of the so-and-sos get past you. Send Finnegan back to me, and move fast or he'll be out in the open in daylight."

I said: "Right – what about some breakfast?"

"You can eat when you're in the new position. Come on now, you're holding up the works."

Turning on my heel I stamped away to the platoon, who were still standing to quietly in the slit trenches. Sergeant Woods made room for me beside him. When I did not speak at first, he turned to Jock Lawson and said in a stage whisper:

"Watch yer 'ealth; young Napoleon's got a liver on."

"Bloody funny! Right, now listen to this: get them to unfix bayonets and follow me. We're going for a walk—now!" Both men groaned. "And another thing. If anyone opens his mouth when you give the order, I'll ram my boot in it."

The men came out silently, looking daggers at me. Woods counted them.

"That's the lot, sir, twenty-eight. Which way—back home?"

"The other end of Satpangon, and I'll lead. Come on." Somebody let out a low whistle.

"Bleedin' sharp end again already! Are we the only sods fighting this lousy war?"

In twenty minutes we had circled back through Wetto and the scrub where I had left Charlie Bates the previous evening. I found that 'D' Company's third platoon had joined them there, brought forward by Freddie Coope, who had succeeded Kitley as Company

Commander. Charles looked a bit sick when I told him where we were going and he led me to a gap in one of the bunds.

"Finnegan went on a bearing of 198 degrees for one thousand paces. He should be in the scrub down on the river bank, but we've not seen hide nor hair of him since he went through last evening." Charles slapped me on the shoulder. "Keep your eyes skinned, Coop. There was an awful lot of shooting over there a couple of hours ago.

We went on cautiously in open file, praying that no enterprising Japs had been out in the night sowing mines or booby-traps for us to walk on.

"978 . . . 979 . . ."

I counted the paces off to myself like a litany. Did Finnegan expect us to relieve him now? Why the hell hadn't Peter mentioned it? God, this is just asking for trouble . . .

A figure rose out of the scrub and I almost died of fright. One got to know a man's silhouette, though, in war. This one registered on my reflexes in a flash . . . *Finnegan*! My finger released the first pressure on the trigger of my rifle with the muzzle a foot from Finnegan's navel. He spoke first.

"I've been watching this bloody back-bearing for hours for someone to come and relieve us."

Finnegan had had quite a night of it. He stabbed with his finger towards the dark scrub.

"The river's just over there and there's three dead Japs on the top of the beach. They came out looking around last night and we gave them all we had, so as the others would think we were here in strength."

Finnegan's six-man patrol had used a 2-inch mortar, grenades and two bren guns to despatch the Japs to their ancestors! The rest of the time they had lain in the open, in a circle, their heels touching, listening uneasily with their eyes playing tricks. Their nerves must have been by that time near breaking-point.

They had found some bone identification sticks, which one of the Japs had concealed in a loin-cloth underneath his uniform trousers. Finnegan's patrol made off almost at a run towards 'D' Company's position, whilst Woods and I roughed out our new posts.

Fortunately the ground there by the river was soft and sandy, so that within half an hour we were pretty well below ground. As the

Eastern sky brightened, I called in the covering screen which I had had out in front while we dug.

The place we had chosen, although some 500 yards from the Japs in Satpangon, was too open for movement between trenches in daylight. There was no shade. It was a question of sitting it out in the sun and making as little movement as possible, in case the Japs saw us and brought their mortars on to us – or possibly their guns across the river.

It had become all too obvious to us by now that a strong, well dug-in force of the enemy was facing us in Satpangon. It had probably been sent across specifically to defend this point, which was the only one for many miles in either direction from which a full-scale assault across the river could be launched. The Satpangon position was what was once known in military parlance as a sally port, and, by placing the Japanese force there, the enemy commander had insured two things. First, that our build-up for an assault crossing of the river would be delayed whilst the area was cleared; and secondly, that his men, with their backs to the river, would have to fight it out to the last. There could be no withdrawal for the Japanese in Satpangon. They were expendable – a suicide force committed to denying us use of the crossing place.

I lay and surveyed this new profile of Satpangon in the early dawn. I complacently reminded myself that we were the only sub-unit on this side of the village and were to be used in any impending attack as a stopping force, to prevent the enemy escaping along the river bank to the west. I still persisted in believing this would be my role even after my signaller gave me a message from Colonel Harvey, who had arrived with his HQ from Myinmu and resumed command. He told me to expect the remainder of 'B' Company to join me at last light.

I could envisage the activity which must have been going on over in Wetto and the area beyond. The men would be cleaning their weapons, preparing breakfast, and speculating as to the particular form which the attack would take. There would be order groups, with artillery forward observation officers fussing about, and the Commanding Officer and Company Commanders poring over aerial photos, if they had any.

Soon the mortars and guns would be ranged. If the Japanese

commander in Satpangon were half as intelligent as the superior who had sent him there, he would be calculating on the basis of past experience just how long it would be before the attack was launched. He would be trying to anticipate from which direction we would come at him.

To fortify a village the size of Satpangon in full, all-round defence in depth, would have required a full-strength British battalion. Well over a thousand men. The Japanese relied, however, on mutually supporting strong-points, with carefully interlaced machine-gun fields of fire, extremely well camouflaged foxholes, bunkers and sniping posts. They used fast-moving counter-attack forces, which they held back from the forward position until they were required. Nevertheless I estimated that even an understrength Japanese battalion would be hard put to it to cover every eventuality at Satpangon. This was a fairly large village, some five or six hundred yards in length, and perhaps three hundred yards from the river bank inland at the deepest point.

At the north-west corner facing my platoon was a bulge of bushes, scrub and heavily foliaged trees. Three gold-leaf pagoda umbrellas stood amongst some taller fringed palm trees in the middle of it. Immediately to the right of this bulge was what appeared to be a gap in the perimeter of the village. I took this to be the western end of the main track or street, which probably ran parallel to the river.

Some fifty to one hundred yards to the right of where I was crouching in the slit trench was the Irrawaddy, across which, almost a mile distant, I could faintly discern through the morning mist the silvery sand of the enemy-held southern shore.

As the sun rose higher in the east above the village, the four or five hundred yards of no-man's-land beyond our scrub-covered trenches began to shimmer in the heat haze. I was struck with the sheer brutality of exotic colour all around: brazen blue of the cloudless sky, red dust, a dozen shades of green and olive in the trees and bushes, the pink and gold pagodas, like the breasts of a delicate woman, peeping through the fan of palm fronds. Overall there had descended a blanket of silence, broken faintly now and then by the unearthly tinkling of the glass bells in the temples.

SEVEN

A New Pair of Boots

I had sited two carefully camouflaged sentry posts slightly forward and to the flanks of my platoon position. These could be relieved with the minimum of movement. I had ordered that no one should show himself above ground, except the sentries, who would have to crawl laboriously into position every two hours.

Smith, Woods and I had dug a fairly substantial trench from which I had the other sections in view. When standing I could see most of the village from the river to the bulge.

We settled down to sweat out the remaining hours until dark, when we would have our first opportunity to move about and relieve our limbs.

Woods took the first watch, and I screwed myself into a corner of the trench to try and sleep. Sun temperatures in Burma at that time of year often reach anything up to 130 degrees, and it was like an oven there in the sandy trench. We had the added discomfort of all kinds of insects, sandflies, and red dust settling on all the exposed parts of our skin.

I awakened cramped and wet through with sweat, with a splitting headache. The sun, like a white hot blast furnace, seemed to fill the sky. After a moment or two things began to focus, but my eyes were playing me tricks. I tried to smoke a cigarette. I was sick. My whole body began to shake with uncontrollable shivers, although I felt as though my skin was frying.

I had had malaria attacks often enough by now to recognize the symptoms, but even the slightest bout of fever in our present predicament was dreadful to contemplate. Smith gave me three mepachrine tablets: they only made me retch and I couln't swallow the vile-tasting things, which stuck somewhere in the back of my throat. Cowering on the bottom of the trench, I must have fallen into a deep sleep again. When I awoke the fever had abated and, as I began to try to ease my cramped and aching limbs, I realised that it was almost dark and the others were standing to arms in deathly quiet. A cool breeze blew wisps of dust into my face and sand trickled slowly off the walls of the trench into my hair. The tinkle of the pagoda bells came faintly through the silence.

Presently Florence crawled over to us from the left-flank sentry position to report that the advance guard of the company had arrived. Shortly afterwards we were joined by the remainder, together with a couple of sections of Indian machine gunners from the Jat Regiment. Peter Clark, the Company second-in-command, came over to see us and I gave him a quick briefing on the layout of my platoon, and in the fading light pointed out as much as I could of the enemy position. Peter showed me some aerial photographs and told me that the bulge in the north-west corner of the village was the Burmese graveyard. Woods told us there had been nothing to report all day, except that one of the relieving sentries thought he had seen a man moving across the track in the village towards the bulge during the afternoon.

I was feeling much better and took the opportunity of returning with Peter to where the Company Commander had established his headquarters at the foot of a large tree, about a hundred yards to the rear. Alistair Falconer was a hefty raw-boned Scot with a fierce moustache, which he had grown to cover a slight disfigurement of his upper lip, where he had been wounded by a Jap bullet earlier in the campaign. He seemed in fairly high spirits and asked me how things had been for the past few days. Before I could tell him, he said that he had a small job for us to do and wanted to put me in the picture quickly, before getting the other platoons laid out. No doubt he thought our twelve hours' turkish bath in the trenches that day had given us sufficient respite to recover from whatever we had done previously. I tried to look as cheerful and nonchalant as I could under the circumstances. Until I heard what he wanted me to do . . .

Apparently it had been decided to send in two fighting patrols: Charlie Bates with a platoon from 'D' Company from the north, and myself with my platoon from the west. We were to do it without initial artillery support – fight our way to the middle of Satpangon and join forces there. Zero hour was fixed for 8 pm, which was in two hours' time. That seemed to be all there was to it. The possibility of Charlie's platoon and mine shooting each other up in the process did not even occur to me at the time. I was still in a very weakened and light-headed state after the fever. In addition the casual and seemingly senseless way in which the fighting patrols had been conceived left me in despair and disbelief.

I left Alistair making himself and his headquarters more comfortable for the night, and returned to my platoon. The men were fine-drawn and sick with fatigue and the heat. The faces I saw before me were haggard and bleary-eyed, traced with dirt and lines of fatigue – dry pinched faces, with a kind of sallow greyness under the young tanned skin and a certain unique, weary resignation in the tired eyes. I saw in them the same sagging fear which numbed my own spirit.

After giving out my orders, I made some banal remark and noticed that only Smith jerked out a cynical, cheerfully blasphemous rejoinder at my pitiful attempt to encourage them. I lay back in the darkness shivering and prayed, waiting for the zero hour.

Somehow I tried to pull myself together and think of the patrol sensibly. Gradually, as the moment drew nearer, my spirits recovered and the despair was replaced by excitement at the prospect of movement and action.

At eight o'clock we moved over towards the enemy village. The night was starlit but not too light. We were able to see each other in shadowy outline as the platoon advanced in a straggling extended order.

No-man's-land seemed interminably wide and full of hidden horrors. We seemed to have covered a great distance when we found ourselves being impaled on short bamboo stakes. The Japs had placed these obstacles in the grass to act as a porcupine fence in front of their positions. They were as sharp as needles, hardened by fire, and planted in such a way that, had we been coming at a run, they would have caused some pretty uncomfortable wounds.

As we picked our way gingerly through these, trying to maintain contact with each other and some sort of formation, the tall trees above the edge of Satpangon suddenly loomed over us in silhouette. We could not have been more than fifty yards away when there was a deafening explosion and a blinding flash. Either a light mortar bomb or a grenade . . . I could not make out. Immediately the night

was ravaged by the crash and rattle of small-arms fire from Satpangon, and tracer bullets lashed through the darkness from half a
dozen directions at once. Most of us found cover behind a paddy
bund not more than eighteen inches high and tried to return the
enemy fire. Lawson and Bullard got up to their usual stunt of firing
2-inch mortar bombs at low angles, hoping no doubt to start a fire,
so that we should be able to see the enemy position more clearly.
Already I had located four machine-guns evenly spaced at points
along the village edge. And over on the left, in the Burmese graveyard, two more had been firing until a moment or two previously.
The Japs' aim must have been high in the darkness and we were not
presenting much of a target. As the fire fight went on, the graveyard
guns opened up again. Those two had us almost in enfilade,
although the tracers were still high and flying out over the river on
our right. Suddenly I realised that the Jap could well be working
some of his men along the river bank, in order to take us on the
right flank. I sent Bill Hughes and a couple of other men, who were
lying nearby, crawling in that direction with a Bren gun to cover us.

The fire fight went on and I was beginning to wonder what to do
next. If we ran on, a good many of us might get to the village. But,
once inside, we would be lost and probably start shooting each
other in the pitch blackness. The Japs were undoubtedly well down
in bunkers and dug-outs, and everything that moved would be hos-
tile to them and treated accordingly. So far I had not heard anything which sounded like an attack from Charlie's side of the
proceedings. If we went on a hundred yards or so, always providing
we got that far, and just lay doggo until daylight, we would be
stranded with 500 yards of open ground behind us. In the flash and
light of the tracers I could see a low mound stretching from end to
end of the edge of the village in front of us. I guessed that, as most
of the automatic fire was coming from there, it must be a gigantic
front-line bunker, probably fifty yards long. I thought of edging
over towards the river bank to try and break in that way. I suggested it to Woods, but he said it was too obvious an approach and
was sure to be well covered.

Our mortaring had had the desired effect, and in one or two
places fires had broken out. In the flickering light the Japs intensified their fire, and one of the machine-guns traversed along the
bund and splattered us with stones and earth.

I could hear Florence shouting to someone and asking where I was. I called out to him and he told me the men were running short on ammunition for the Brens, and that all the 2-inch bombs were finished.

Suddenly there was a lull in the firing and then we heard the wuppering shriek of mortar-bombs falling through the air. I have always had a sneaking suspicion that they were our own 3-inch mortars firing. They came down in front of us between the bund and the graveyard, but they were too close for comfort. I think it was at this point that I decided the whole business was a shambles and we might as well pull out. Billy Hughes' Bren gun began hammering away near the river bank. Somebody yelled that the Japs were coming out that way.

I told Sergeant Woods to withdraw the left-flank section back to the Company position. Two minutes later I passed the word for the others to retire after them.

Our withdrawal was almost a panic, men crawling, falling and cursing at their weapons and equipment in their eagerness to get away. More firing broke out from the river bank and the crack-thump and zip of bullets and screaming metal from the bursting mortar-bombs ripped through the air round our heads as we stumbled towards the trenches.

Miraculously our casualties were light. Only three of the men were lightly wounded and Corporal Murray missing. He remained out only about thirty yards from the Japs in the Burmese graveyard for several hours and crawled back to our lines during the night. He had been knocked senseless by either a flying stone or shrapnel which had slammed into his waist-belt buckle. He was very shaken and his limbs shivered uncontrollably when they brought him to me. He said the Japs had been wandering around him in the paddy-fields and he thought his number was up.

When I reported to Alistair, he seemed not in the least concerned about our failure to get right into the village and insisted that I stay at his HQ for a while. He gave me some rum while I told him as much as I could concerning the positions of the Jap bunkers and of the machine guns. Back at my platoon I lay down in a trench with my half blanket around my head to try and keep the mosquitoes at bay.

Some time later the artillery began harassing the Jap positions and occasional flashes split the darkness of the trench. Twisting and turning fitfully in an effort to sleep, my mind still occupied with searing pictures of the abortive raid, I suddenly became fully awake, sweating, tense.

Woods, who had been on watch, had come back to the trench. He reported movement along the river bank. I went with him to one of the Bren posts. The moon was up. In the shadow of the high sandy bank above the beach we saw stealthy figures moving towards us.

Crawling close to Cheeseborough, the Bren gunner, I whispered to him to await my order to fire. He nodded and settled his cheek into the butt of the gun.

Moments passed. I remember fighting with the idea that these things approaching were not men at all, but inhuman beings, beyond the reach of ordinary mortals.

Jerkily the figures climbed up the river bank and fanned out thirty yards away, coming closer. The lever of a grenade pinged away into the scrub with Woods shouting:

"Share that, you bastards!"

The Japs hesitated. I tapped Cheeseborough on the shoulder. The Bren gun hammered out as I fired a Very light into the face of the nearest enemy soldier. A burst of automatic fire splattered into the sand around us and immediately the earsplitting explosion of Woods's grenade split the night in two. The Japs began to spin and jerk like marionettes. One of them walked almost casually away from the others and then there was a blinding flash and we saw him fleetingly in the glare, a heap of rags and threshing limbs draped across a bush. One of the Bren bullets must have hit a grenade in his belt.

We lay sweating, every nerve-end aching and our bodies stiff with fear and excitement. But there was no sound or movement.

Cheeseborough's Number Two threw another grenade. We waited for a moment or two, then walked hesitantly forward towards the crumpled bodies. One of the Japs was holding his face in his hands; another was kneeling as though kow-towing. Woods kicked the body sideways, covering it with his bayonet.

There had been seven Japanese in the patrol and they were all dead.

Alistair was like a dog with two tails when I reported to him.

"Pity you didn't get one of them alive, though," he said.

When I got back to the platoon, Bullard brought me a pair of boots which he had taken from one of the dead Japs. He had cut through the laces with a razor blade. He was wearing a clean khaki shirt himself, which he had looted from one of the Japanese haversacks. Smith told me later that Bull had also added to his collection of gold teeth. How he managed to prise these out of the mouths of dead Japs I never learnt. His ghoulish activities were barely given a second thought by any of us. In fact we thought it quite a joke. I could not help chuckling to myself at the grotesque way he had provided me with new boots. My own had long since worn through to the uppers.

For a while during the remainder of the night Jap mortar bombs whirred down into the scrub beyond the Jat machine-gunners who were dug in close to the river bank on our right flank. The Jats had a disconcerting habit of wandering about between their weapon pits at all hours and it was a wonder none of them was hit. Later on a dozen or so Jap shells came over but seemed to land anywhere but on us . . . mercifully!

Before stand-to we drank the remains of the water in our bottles and replenished them from the Irrawaddy. The night had been trying and we were restless and tired. Half the platoon, in turns, had been standing to ever since we had clobbered the Jap patrol.

At first light, when everybody was on his feet, I was summoned to Company HQ for an Orders Group of Platoon Commanders. On the way the frogs, crickets and tree-rats began to make a shocking din, as they greeted the new day. Prowling jackals provided an *obbligato*.

Alistair Falconer was writing notes in his field-message pad with some difficulty in the half light. The other two Platoon Commanders, Sergeant Cassels and Sergeant O'Neil, were already with the Company Commander and all three greeted me as I approached. Waiting until I had settled myself on the ground, cradling my rifle across my knees, Alistair came straight to the point.

"This afternoon at 1400 hours we are attacking Satpangon."

As the portent of this opening sentence sank in, resentment and disbelief welled up, then changed sharply to cold fear. My limbs grew weak and began to tremble. I realised that I was missing – had missed – the greater part of the detail of Alistair's orders. I heard his voice droning on.

The assault was to be limited to a frontage of one platoon, with two sections forward and one back. Sergeant O'Neil's platoon was detailed as the first wave, with the bunker and defended locality in the Burmese graveyard as its objective. My platoon was to follow up immediately, swing right at the graveyard and then roll up the vast bunker I had seen at close quarters in the night. It ran from north to south between the track and the river at the edge of the village.

Company HQ would come in behind us. When we were in the village, Peter Clark was to bring the third platoon forward with picks and shovels, reserve ammunition and the Jat machine-gunners. We were then to consolidate fifty yards inside the village.

We were to have 3-inch mortar, artillery and air support. While the initial assault on the graveyard was in progress, the Jat machine-gunners were to provide covering fire by strafing the edge of the village from the track to the beach. At last the orders were complete and we synchronised watches. The dress for the attack was to be 'field service marching order', which meant in fact everything we owned. With weapons and ammunition this was a load of 40 or 50 pounds, and it seemed to me that the powers-that-be must have thought it would be literally a walkover.

The Burma dawn brought full light in about twenty minutes, and Smith and I hurried back to our trenches.

Considering the information I had reported during the night concerning the size and strength of the enemy positions facing us, with goodness knew what else in depth behind, it seemed to me particularly stupid to attack in the hottest part of the day, weighed down with all our baggage, across a five-hundred-yard paddyfield, as bare of cover as a billiard table. The bunker on the edge of Satpangon, facing my platoon's position, was the biggest I had ever seen, and those in the graveyard must be a fair size, though I hadn't seen them closely.

Japanese 'bunkers' were deep dug-outs roofed with layers of tree-trunks, covered with four or five feet of earth. They were so well camouflaged that they couldn't be picked out easily at even fifty yards. They held garrisons of varying numbers, usually from five to twenty, but sometimes even as many as a hundred or more. The bunkers were constructed with a series of loopholes covering cleared fields of fire, and designed to house light and medium belt-fed machine-guns. When completed, these strongholds were impervious to mortar and shell-fire and could even withstand 250-pound aerial bombs. Armour-piercing anti-tank shells were the only missiles which could really inflict damage on them. Infantry on their own had somehow to penetrate close enough to lob phosphorus bombs or Mills grenades through the loopholes. Pole-charges (or Bangalore torpedoes) were occasionally used to demolish the bunkers, but I had never seen them in use.

Bunkers were always sited in groups giving mutual support, so that troops assaulting them could rarely reach one without coming under fire from at least two others. Apart from this there were the cunning little sods in foxholes covering every approach to the bunker. Whenever our troops did manage to reach them, the Japanese defensive technique was to mortar, shell and machine-gun their own positions, irrespective of any damage they might inflict on their own men in the process. They weren't likely to do much damage to the Japs in the bunkers opposite us, that was for sure.

I shuddered at the off-hand way in which the attack was being organised. It certainly would never have done at the battle schools in England! As we crawled into the trench, I did not dare to look Smith in the face. Sergeant Woods, the nonchalant, the reckless, went on cleaning his rifle, oblivious to what was in store for us.

Smith began to prepare breakfast while I made a few notes on the orders that I would give to the platoon.

After the meal I had the Section Commanders crawl over to us and told them all they must know.

When I finished and asked the usual "Any questions?", I expected my two sergeants – no respecters of persons at the best of times – to let fly with all my own unspoken queries and bitter comments:

"Why 'B' Company? Or at any rate, why us? When were the other bastards going to do something? Bloody suicide attack! Hadn't I put them in the picture about the bunkers and the machine guns? . . ." and so on and so on.

Alistair had said he wanted Sergeant Florence with his HQ in the attack, because the CSM had gone to Battalion HQ during the night and had not yet returned. I told him this now, partly to divert the NCOs from any further mutinous mutterings.

Woods, who had not said much, eventually became as cheerful as ever and began to sing in a cracked voice:

> Kiss me goodnight, Sergeant-Major.
> Sergeant-Major be a mother to me.

Florence, who was gathering his equipment together, grinned sheepishly and told him to "get stuffed!"

That being that, we settled down to getting everything ready. As Florence began crawling away back to Company HQ, he looked round at us and said:

"Don't forget that Yankee blanket of yours – you promised it to me if you went west, Lakri."

Sergeant Woods grinned and flung a clump of earth at him. Personally I felt like a condemned man waiting for the hangman and their attempt at nonchalance was lost on me. I seemed to have used up all my bravado long since. I was as jumpy as a cat. And yet I felt heavy with sleep. This is often the case in action, presumably because of the intense mental strain.

During the next few hours there were spasmodic exchanges of rifle shots and machine-gun bursts between the enemy and the companies over the eastern side of Satpangon. Perhaps a little fire-fight had been laid on over there by way of diverting the attention of the Japanese from ourselves.

As the time for the attack drew near my training and reflexes seemed to take over and my brain worked overtime.

Finally I adjusted my equipment, wound my watch, set my steel helmet at the lucky angle, pulled the entrenching tool in its webbing case round in front – not that it would stop anything, but it helped psychologically.

I took the Mills grenades out of my pouch and secured them by the levers on the back of my belt. I put two spare clips of cartridges into my right-hand trouser pocket. All set. I found myself blaspheming at everyone in sight and my jaw muscles ached trying to keep a smile on my face.

EIGHT

Satpangon – Profile of a Battle

We had been glad that the attack would be unusually strongly supported, both by aircraft and artillery. It was to be a divisional concentration of guns – a most impressive affair, whilst it was taking place, and even rather effective after all the dust had settled. The sweat dripped down from the linings of our steel helmets and into our eyes. Our throats were parched, but we smoked incessantly.

The promised barrage opened directly from the north. It exceeded our wildest expectations. The air was suddenly filled with a great swishing and rushing, as tons of steel hurtled towards the great wood that shrouded Satpangon.

There was a ragged array of red and yellow flashes from the trees. A great thunder of high explosive struck our ears. Billows of black, blue and dirty yellow smoke and dust rolled slowly skywards. And still more deadly cylinders of steel whispered through the air on their way to the target.

It seemed as though the whole village must already be flattened behind that wall of smoke.

Then the shelling ended, the smoke began to clear and there stood Satpangon, seemingly as it had always stood, sullen, evil and unrevealing.

A fresh delivery of friendly steel went hissing over. There was another violent inferno and another curtain of smoke. Solid lumps of something shot up into the sky.

Satpangon appeared the same as before when the smoke lifted, however, and waited for its next salvo of shells and the next . . . and the next . . .

There was just one thing wrong, however. The bombardment had started and would end just twenty minutes too early.

"Get up, get up – move out now! Now!"

Alistair was behind us, running towards us in the open.

"Get your platoon moving straight away, Cooper. Shake out as you go!"

There was obviously no time to ask the reason why. We were going, and that was it.

Unprepared, the NCOs and I began staggering out of the trenches, dragging our packs and weapons. The heat was appalling. We harried and chivvied the men out of the sweltering trenches and pressed them into some sort of battle formation.

Sergeant O'Neil's platoon was already moving out alongside us on our left and, as I remembered the orders, I tried to make some readjustment so that we could get over behind them. Alistair, kneeling in the rear with his runner and signallers, bellowed to me to forget about the formation and get on. We found ourselves plodding forward in an extended line about 150 yards wide, both platoons alongside each other with bayonets fixed. I thought of the machine-guns in the bunkers ahead and my stomach turned over.

This was going to be a 'blitz' attack then . . . despite the carefully ordered plan – a head-on, lined-up charge at whatever got in our way.

I thought of my father and my two uncles on the Somme in the First World War when, with their battalion of Fusiliers, they had charged the German machine-guns on 1st July 1916.

'Blitzing', in the infantry in Burma, meant you advanced on at least a platoon front at a quick walking pace with all guns blazing. It is the old 'death or glory' stuff, usually reserved for close jungle fighting.

But we had five hundred yards to go before we could begin our blitz. Five hundred yards of a Somme walk at the high port.

After a moment or two firing came from the right rear and bullets swished by. The Jat machine-gunners had got into action, quite deliberately and without flurry, and were making an infernal noise too close for comfort.

On we went, and then rocket-firing Hurricanes screamed down out of the western sky low over our heads. In line abreast, by flights of three aircraft, the Indian Air Force squadron swooped towards the smoking village. As they pulled up and hurtled away north-wards, their bombs smashed and battered into the trees. Round and back they came, this time in line – astern, with machine-guns and rockets blazing. Most of the way across no-man's-land they were with us, drawing us forward and on towards the enemy. They strafed so low as to seem to disappear for seconds at a time into the smoking chaos of the blazing woods. Then, as suddenly as they had appeared, they were gone, all except one which zoomed over us twice more without firing. Presumably, all ammunition gone, he had stayed to give us moral support across the last couple of hundred yards.

When he finally waggled his wings and flew after the squadron, we felt alone and naked. Alone with nothing between us and the enemy except our jutting bayonets.

Suddenly we were in the pungi sticks, close to the low bund where we had fought the Japanese in our abortive raid during the night.

So sudden, so infinitesimal in time, is the crash of an explosion, that events which are simultaneous with it seem seconds long and quite divorced by comparison. First there was the sensation of a sudden stinging slap in the face, and a curious momentary sense of elation came over me. I realised that I had flung myself onto my face, that my rifle had almost buried itself in the dust six feet ahead, that my mouth was hot and sticky with blood, and that Corporal Buckley and at least two other members of my platoon lay dead or dying.

Scrambling to my feet and recovering my rifle, I heard the Jap machine-guns firing from the edge of the village. I saw Private Gammie, one of Buckley's men, running back towards our lines, blood flowing from his neck and bawling that he had been hit by the lousy yellow bastards.

Immediately in front, near the entrance to the main street of the village, two or three Japanese were manning a machine-gun in full view. The gun was firing without stopping – the ammunition belt writhing and leaping like a tortured snake.

Both O'Neil's platoon and mine were flat on their faces, hypnotised by the flash of guns and the hiss of flailing bullets.

I remember waving my arm rather theatrically and shouting:

"Come on, Come on."

But no one moved. The nearest man to me was Barrett. Brave as any man though I knew him to be, nevertheless I rushed at him like a green-clad dervish.

"Up, up, get up or I'll blow your brains out."

He looked up at me in disbelieving astonishment. Something snapped inside my head and I found myself running wildly towards the enemy machine-guns . . . alone.

As I ran I fired my rifle from the hip and continued to do so even after I realised that the bullets were merely kicking up red dust a dozen yards in front of me. I paused in my headlong race and saw Thomas, our wild Liverpool Welshman, who had appeared as if from nowhere, a few yards to my right. Barrett was there too. They were howling like banshees . . . and then they were all with me. My platoon came in like a cyclone. Just before we reached the Japanese bunker everyone began firing at once. We were running flat out like maniacs, and everything was being fired from the hip – rifles, Brens, Stens. Bullets were streaking everywhere into and around us and ripping into the undergrowth, the bunker and the bamboo huts beyond.

Seconds later I saw Peggy O'Neil's men going through the grave-yard on our left in a crashing torrent of fire. Then I no longer saw them. There were too many huts and trees in the way, too much bamboo and too much smoke, and I realised that we were over the bunker and amongst the enemy foxholes.

Behind me, around and on top of the bunker, was a seething mass of cursing men locked in an infernal noise of screams and detonations. Phosphorus bombs were exploding in the bunker and the Japs were coming out, burning alive. Smith appeared beside me, and there were two sharp bursts of light-machine-gun fire from somewhere up in the trees.

Isherwood ran up alongside us luggging his Bren gun and then, out of a hole under the nearest hut, scrambled a naked Burmese woman, fat and demented. Screaming as she ran towards us, she fell at our feet with a great bloodstain on her face and head.

There were enemy foxholes all around us. Fires were spreading into the huts and roaring up the tree-trunks. The blazing bamboo exploded with the noise of gun shots, augmenting the already deafening din. The flames were almost on us and we could feel the searing heat.

Isherwood's Bren hammered madly. Through the smoke about thirty yards away, running towards us like sprinters, came two Jap officers brandishing swords above their heads. Behind them came more Japanese.

A group of us began hurling grenades and phosphorus bombs into the mass of howling Japs. As the smoke mushroomed up about them, the enemy counter-attack faltered and the yammer of firing died down momentarily. A figure rushed out of the smoke and I recognised Cecil Jotham followed by about half a dozen men from O'Neil's platoon.

"Pegg's been hit," he yelled. "Christ knows how many more as well."

I gave them orders to take up all-round defence and we tried to get into some sort of organised position with the village blazing all around us.

There were no Japs left in the immediate vicinity except dead ones, but there were obviously plenty of others to take us on, and, as far as I could make out, only twenty of us left from both platoons to hold what we had gained so far. A good many had been hit before we got to the bunkers, and Woods said he had seen O'Neil and some others making their way back wounded to our own lines.

Firing broke out again, mostly from the bunker in the grave-yard which O'Neil's platoon had overrun. As we returned the fire, I saw Isherwood in the open space of the village street. Smith was a few feet away from him with a handful of Bren pouches, feeding the gun with fresh magazines.

I shouted to them to drop back to the bunker. As they got up to do so, Isherwood was knocked over with a bullet in the leg and a grenade burst wounded Smith in the shoulder.

Rushing to them, furious that they had been shooting from such a conspicuous position, I pulled Isherwood and the Bren gun into a deep bomb crater nearby, with Smith's help.

I fully expected that we would be joined any minute by Company HQ and Peter with the reserve platoon. The minutes went by and the firing intensified, and still they did not appear.

Isherwood was mumbling something about a grenade. I began to take out his field dressing. Then I realised that he did in fact have a 36 grenade in one of his trouser pockets. The Jap bullet had smashed the bomb into fragments without exploding it. I felt gingerly about, found the fuse and threw it over the lip of the crater. Ripping Isherwood's trousers, I slapped his field dressing over the hole in his leg, which looked pretty shocking with bits of metal from the grenade embedded in it.

There was a shout, and Florence hurtled over the edge of the crater in a flurry of dust and a burst of machine-gun fire. I rolled over to make room for him and as I did so I saw for the first time a Japanese sniper on a tree platform thirty feet above our heads. He was trying to bring a light automatic to bear so that he could fire vertically down on us where we lay almost directly below him in the bomb crater. How anyone could have survived up there is a mystery I shall never unravel. Smith saw the Jap at the same moment and fired a burst from his Sten from where he lay on his back beside us. I saw Alistair: he was yelling at Woods behind the bunker and asking him where I was. In all the noise and smoke and general confusion I don't suppose that Alistair had noticed the tree sniper any more than we had. The next moment I saw him running towards us, crouching low. He saw us when he was a few steps from the crater.

"Well done, well done," he shouted. "Get back out of it as soon as you can – we can't hold this position. . . ."

The rest of the sentence was drowned by the rat-a-tat of the tree sniper's gun. The burst took Alistair in the head and shoulders. He fell as though smashed into the ground by a pile-driver. The next thing I knew, Smith and I were out in the open dragging Alistair's heavy weight between us. Florence belting away with his rifle at the Jap up above, who seemed to have a charmed life.

Somehow we managed to get Alistair into a deep L-shaped trench in a flurry of sand and muck. I tipped the Company Commander's steel hat back and for a little he breathed noisily as his bloody head flopped against my chest. Then he seemed to stop breathing. He lay quiet and grey, with foam and blood over his moustache. No sound came from him; but his eyes were staring and his lips moved up and down. I think I felt there might be hope, so I placed a couple of morphine tablets under his tongue and Smith poured a little water into his mouth.

Mortar bombs were dropping more often now. The blast and the horrible whine of flying fragments slashed at my nerves. Great lumps of earth fell into the trench.

Someone was screaming:

"Do something, do something. For Christ's sake, do something."

The sky seemed to fall into the trench and I swear the trench itself moved in the ground. There was a battering yet piercing screech in my head and all the breath seemed to blast out of my lungs through my ears.

The Jap tree sniper was in the trench on top of us. The sky seemed to rain dust and chunks of burning wood and ashes.

How I came to be with the others back near the Jap bunker, I never knew, but somebody must have dragged me. Lawson and Bullard were leaning over me and my head ached abominably.

We seemed to be in a corner on one side of the bunker, where it formed a T-junction. The Japanese in the graveyard were as active as ever. Behind us in the paddyfield on the other side of the bunker I could hear somebody wailing, screaming. Out there one of our own dead had awakened. He was calling now, pitifully, uselessly. From across the river the Japanese were firing infantry guns. Whizz bangs. Their target was probably the walking wounded, who were crawling and staggering back across no-man's-land. The Japs were still watching from cover deeper into Satpangon. Some of the men could see movements amongst the foliage, although it was very hazy with the smoke and dust from the shelling.

Ten yards behind us in the paddy lay an unexploded 250-pound bomb from the air-strike. Jap shells were dropping perilously close to it. A phosphorus grenade was burning with volumes of white smoke some yards away: the fumes nearly choked us.

I couldn't make up my mind what to do. Peter Clark and the reserve platoon had not come. Nor would they come now, I felt sure. They had given us up for dead, or the enemy guns had them pinned down. What could I do? There were only two options. To stay in Satpangon was something I hardly dared think about. If we tried to get back to the Company position, the Japs in the grave-yard would make mincemeat of us on the way.

Then I heard a too-familiar whizzing noise again and realised that our own 3-inch mortars were firing into the graveyard and the pagodas. The bedlam of noise seemed to rebound like a solid weight off the other side of the bunker, smashing and echoing from the gross impact.

"*Banzai! Banzai!*" The screams were distinct and struck terror into my heart.

The Japanese were moving in for another counter-attack. They were coming down the axis of the main street and through the undergrowth on either side.

We began to fire at them as they dodged and weaved amongst the trees and burning huts. Two of our Brens were still in action. As they continued to bellow and traverse I wondered how long the ammunition would last. A tall Japanese officer ran across the street twenty or thirty yards away. He reappeared with a bunch of ragged-looking yellow men behind him. They came straight at us, apparently oblivious of the furious blizzard of steel which was screaming about them.

They were just running straight into it – unconcerned, uncaring – as though each man were an inviolate demi-god – running into the flailing cones of bullets and mortar-bomb explosions like fiends, confident of passing unscathed. And somehow, because the sight had so much of its own unique and uncanny terror, for a moment I experienced a weird shock of total panic. I almost believed that these figures were indeed more than human, and that they could advance unhurt – fantastic beings to whom bullets and shells were harmless, who would come on and on until they reached us at the bunker.

And then they were not there any more. There was only the monstrous crash of shells: they could have been ours or theirs. I didn't care any more. Then there was a sudden and incredible silence, except for the crackling flames. Smoke billowed all around.

I tried once again to make up my mind what to do, but I was utterly exhausted. I shouted to a man in a crater nearby and recognised Henderson the Company Commander's signaller. Woods yelled at me:

"The buggers got the wireless set."

I struggled to force my mind through the swamp of numbness, fighting desperately to think clearly. My limbs were shuddering uncontrollably. There was a flat, almost ridiculous little crack from out of the smoke somewhere up high, and what seemed like the impact of a stone on Henderson's steel helmet. Why didn't he get up out of the crater and join us! I looked again: his head had dropped and there was a clean round hole in the top of his helmet.

I knew then that we had to attempt a break-out back to the Company lines, whatever the cost. We had no choice; and the next counter-attack by the Japs would take us all.

There were about fifteen men, including a few wounded. We

gathered all the phosphorus grenades we could find into two haversacks.

I told Florence that I would try to cover the run back on the graveyard flank with smoke and Sergeant Woods said he would do the same in the rear. Within minutes we were ready. I stood up, ran a few paces towards the track and flung my first smoke bomb. As the white smoke billowed up, it mixed with the smoke from the burning huts and undergrowth. The men scrambled over the bunker and began to run. I remember Jones stuck close to me. Immediately the vicious crack-thump and zip of rifle and machine-gun fire began again. Faintly I heard Japanese voices shouting – shrill, almost feminine, voices out of the shimmering haze and the smoke.

The glare out on the flat paddy was white-hot. The dust and choking phosphorus smoke swirled around us. Then the whizz and crash of the Jap gunfire coming over the river began again.

We were running, crouching, ducking. Jones almost crashed into me, as he spun out of a cloud of smoke, holding bloody hands to his face. He fell at my feet. I reached a low bund and came upon Sutton lying behind it. I heard him calling to a group of wounded who were being helped along by some others:

"Don't bloody panic, don't bloo . . ." – and then a shell burst a few feet away and knocked me flat, scrabbling in the sand.

I got up, feeling strangely sleepy, almost doped. It was as if suddenly nothing mattered any more. All I knew was that I was desperately thirsty.

My right leg was very painful, but otherwise I seemed to be in one piece. I felt in my haversack for more smoke bombs, but I had used them all.

As my head cleared I saw Sam Steel, a lad of nineteen from the other platoon. He ran past me back towards the graveyard screaming. I thought he must be off his head, but forgot about him almost immediately. I barely had strength to move. Stumbling over Sutton's body, I dragged myself half sitting, half crawling back through the drifting smoke.

After what seemed hours I heard voices calling and saw figures moving about. One of them came towards me and I recognised the Doctor. He gave me some water and I felt his hands examining my chest and leg.

"You'll be OK. Do you think you can make it without my help? There's some badly wounded over here."

I nodded and watched him walk away with some stretcher-bearers. The scene that greeted me amongst the scrub and hillocks and trenches of the Company positions flashed deeply into my consciousness in an instant of vivid detail. The picture was driven into my eye and imprinted indelibly on my memory.

Smith lying against the Command Post tree, his right arm limp by his side. Woods staggering towards the trenches supporting a man round the waist. Peggy O'Neil lying grey-faced on a stretcher, his eyes closed. The crouching shapes of the reserve platoon, and the black mouths of the foxholes and trenches in the scrub.

Near the river bank, a hundred yards away, the Indian soldiers were firing their Vickers machine-guns at the enemy 75s across the river. Near me was a line of silent, blanket-covered forms: booted feet, lying limply at odd angles, protruded from the ends of some of the blankets. Peter Clark was kneeling beside a field telephone. He looked up at me.

"Ken, you've had a nasty job – do you think we could take them in again? I've had only a few casualties here."

Dumbfounded, almost stunned at his suggestion, I managed hoarsely:

"Why didn't you bring in the third platoon when you could see we had a foothold?"

He seemed to weigh my question carefully before answering. Then sadly, with eyes averted, he said haltingly:

"I'm desperately sorry. Those bloody guns had us taped, and we thought you had had it anyhow."

Suddenly I lost interest and walked away to where I had seen Smithie. Snipers' bullets cracked and thumped, but I wanted the comforting presence of my old friend and didn't even bother to duck my head. Dick Florence was with him and, as I flung myself on the ground beside them, he asked me if I was hit. My face and arms were covered with blood. But most of that was Alistair's.

Smithie divided his cigarettes between us and then quietly handed me a grubby air-letter card.

"Sorry, boss, this came up with some mail in the night, but I forgot about it. The rest of it was never given out. There's not many will be needing it now anyway, is there?"

"Any idea what the score is, Dick?" I asked Florence.

"No idea," he answered. "They tell me your mate, Charlie Bates, is badly wounded – sniper got him in the head."

Feeling stiff and drowsy and utterly exhausted, I lay back and idly opened my letter. It was from my mother – dated one week earlier. I read the first eight words only. I could not see the rest: my eyes were clouded with tears.

"Dear son, your father died peacefully this morning . . ."

The wounded were evacuated at last light. After dark Peter Clark, who had assumed command of the Company, sent me with Sergeant O'Connor to reconnoitre the Burmese graveyard in Satpangon. Large fires had broken out amongst the trees there. The crawl across no-man's-land was a heart-stopping experience for me which I was barely capable of carrying out, even though Busty O'Connor lead for most of the way. When we reached the edge of some elephant grass, close enough to see into the graveyard, we were confronted with a scene of the most intimidating and haunting weirdness. Clearly the flickering flames of large fires illuminated a devilish Shinto ritual being carried out amongst the shattered trees and ruined buildings. We watched the Japanese throwing corpses onto the fires – their own dead and ours.

Later still Bob Broach, the company cook corporal, went with me to the river, where we spent the remaining hours of darkness filling mule panniers with water between long bursts of enemy machine-gun fire which lashed the shore line along the Company's right flank. By dawn the water had been distributed round the slit trenches, and we stood to as the sun cut across the sky – a bitter, brilliant, golden shaft, striking the shattered trees of Satpangon and the Japanese stronghold still hidden below them.

At midday several batteries of our twenty-five pounders began firing from the north, regularly splitting the air with a solid smash of flame and noise. Beyond the village rifle and machine-gun fire broke out, and we knew then that the companies from Wetto were attacking Satpangon.

Towards evening we heard the news that Peter Gillam and 'C' Company had gained a foothold and that Terry Hodgson had passed 'A' Company through them and was digging in. Leading the initial assault by 'C' Company my friend, Tommy Turner, was killed at the head of his platoon, most of whom were mown down around him by the cross-fire of the enemy machine-guns which swept no-man's-land like a scythe.

Throughout the night the battle raged inside the village. Near dawn we heard cheering. Loud, hollow, abrupt explosions were followed by the call of a bugle, and then a solid sheet of crackling small-arms fire broke out.

As the sun climbed up behind Satpangon, we watched with incredulous astonishment as a squad of fully armed and equipped Japanese, marching as though on parade, emerged from the burning village. Down they went, like sleep-walking automata, across the gleaming expanse of sunlit beach and on into the rushing water of the Irrawaddy. As their threshing figures were swept towards us in the racing current, the Jat machine-gunners cut loose at point-blank range.

Gathering our last reserves of strength, we stumbled across the corpse-strewn fields and through the Burmese graveyard into Satpangon. Among the rubble, beneath the ruined pagodas and burnt-out bashas the dead of the Battalion sprawled around the bunkers they had silenced; the living lay among them speechless, worn out, beyond anything, and watched with sunken eyes as we joined them.

NINE

Burials and Boat Drill

Robin Gordon pulled me up from the ground and punched and kicked me into wakefulness.

"It's nearly dawn – stand to."

The light, although feeble and grey, slashed into my eyes and I groaned and sank down again.

"Bugger stand-to! To hell with the Japs! To hell with you!" Around me a handful of men were groaning awake. Our enemy was no longer the Japanese, but the dawn light, the weight of our bodies, our equipment and weapons and our sore feet. We were exhausted and past caring. All we wanted was sleep. Wearily we stood to somehow, our heads nodding, leaning on the parapets of the trenches, half dozing as the light grew stronger, our eyes squinting and itching, feet amongst the scarlet flowers fallen from the flame trees in the powdered dust. The only sounds were the sighs and groans of exhaustion and, now and then, a faint bump as someone fell asleep across the mounds of earth and branches surrounding the slit trenches.

As the day came, we peered with red-rimmed eyes at the carnage around us. The stench of putrefying and burnt flesh was indescribable, the village a charred and burnt-out ruin. We were unimpressed. All we desired was to fall once more onto the scorched earth and close our eyes. We were beyond the reach of anything, dead beat.

After stand-down we were left to ourselves for an hour or two, during which the men dropped to the bottom of the fox-holes, asleep before they hit the ground.

A mug of tea and Victory V cigarettes revived the feeble spark of life in us eventually. As we sipped the sickly brew, the smell of iodine, which always pervaded the Japanese trenches and bunkers, reminded us of where we were and how we got there.

Peter Clark came across to inform me of the burial arrangements. The Battalion HQ men had prepared shallow graves in the middle of the village and a padre from Brigade was already there waiting to conduct the service. I had hoped the companies would be switched round to carry each other's dead, but it seemed that this had been overlooked or else the padre was in a hurry, leaving no time for that.

We had found Sammy Steel's body lying across one of the loopholes in the graveyard bunker. Alistair was still in the Jap slit-trench where we had left him when we withdrew: the tree-sniper who had killed him lay across him.

Shelling started again as we began the task of wrapping the dead in their blankets. It was necessary for close friends to make the identification in many cases. Few men wore their identification discs in the prescribed manner, round their necks on a string. I had discarded my own months before, because the piece of string always chafed my neck in that climate.

'B' Company's dead could have been mistaken for giant negroes: their whole bodies were swollen and bloated, bellies bursting through the uniforms. The skin had a deep purple hue to it after the men had lain for so long in the scorching sun. But we heard that Corporal Andrews of 'D' Company was still alive when he was found. A wooden bullet had lodged in the back of his neck. His eyes were wide open. He was blind. He had lain paralysed staring at the sun for five days.

Boots and equipment were removed, letters and personal effects dropped into empty sandbags. The blankets were then sewn up, using pull-throughs and boot laces, after which we carried the bodies towards a clearing in the middle of Satpangon.

When we got into the clearing we found a bare-headed little man standing amongst rows of bundled inert figures. As we approached, he turned and came towards us. My carrying party halted: the stranger walked slowly round us, inspecting us from various angles. Holding his hand across his breast with an air of studious piety he gazed at us; then in an accent thick with Liverpudlian Irish he spoke:

"You're the first walking corpses I've ever had." Then sadly: "Shove your mates in bed here, lads, for me to deal with."

The carrying parties, filthy and exhausted as they were, stood stiffly to attention as though on ceremonial parade. The chaplain read the words of the burial service.

"Hey! Did you know that bloke was a Holy Roman?" This from Rowlands who had been brought up a staunch Baptist in his little Welsh mining village.

"Don't care a bugger," said Florence. "As far as I'm concerned, it don't matter if he's RC, Parsee or even bleeding Khaki. He stayed and buried our lads, didn't he?"

Wearily, apathetically, we handed over the Satpangon perimeter to a battalion of Gurkhas and marched eight miles north to Kandaw Tank.

There were various villages in this part of Burma marked 'Tank' on our maps. We assumed this was due to the ponds, lakes, reservoirs, or just simply mud holes one was likely to find in these particular places. Kandaw had a fairly large, shallow lake, which we found was to be used by us for practising boat-drill.

We settled ourselves in quickly, each platoon digging its own particular sector of the battalion's perimeter trenches. We established a steady routine for ourselves, in contrast to the chaos of the preceding couple of weeks. We took the opportunity of sorting out our tangled and filthy belongings, and within a day or so transformed ourselves into a more passable resemblance of an organised military body.

Spare equipment and personal effects in kit-bags was magically produced by our long-lost 'Admin. Company', who seemed to be always just behind wherever we happened to be. Most of us helped ourselves to spare items of clothing and footwear from the kit-bags and bed-rolls of the men who had fallen or those who had become casualties. We knew that the chances of their next of kin or anyone closer than ourselves getting such things was marginal. Of course small items of a more personal and private nature were replaced and carefully marked, in the hope that relatives would finally receive them.

A piece of ground was cleared and flattened for use as a light-aircraft landing strip. Brigade headquarters established themselves in another village some short distance from us, and for a day or two left us in comparative peace and quiet to lick our wounds and reorganise.

From an air drop of supplies we were issued with things like tinned fruit, razor blades, chocolate, toothpaste, soap and writing materials. These 'comforts' helped tremendously to raise our moral, but nothing more so than a backlog of mail from home, along with some copies of the forces' newspaper, *SEAC*. All of us spent a great deal of time reading everything over and over again. To see the change which came over a man when he was savouring the knowledge of an unopened letter in his pocket from mother, wife or sweetheart was a revelation. Those unfortunates who had failed to receive mail were sometimes allowed to read the letters of their mates – a gesture which demonstrated the close bond and brotherly union existing between these men.

We began to march across to the 'Tank' each day for boat-drill. The folding canvas boats were sorry-looking craft which were not too serviceable, and many of them leaked at the seams. We practised loading and paddling the nine and fourteen-men boats across the lake, and drilled ourselves in the use of Mae West life-belts, which each of us was to wear for the crossing of the Irrawaddy when it came.

Crews and paddlers were detailed off. Dry rehearsals were carried out, so that we could ultimately have formed a bridge-head with our eyes closed. We were due to do so in the dark, anyway, so it was just as well so much time was spent on it. Everything down to the minutest detail was explained over and over. But I am afraid our aptitude for sailing and rowing was low. This turned the edge of our otherwise high degree of skill and preparedness. A boat would be loaded with men and equipment. The order would be given:

"Port, back paddle! Starboard, row."

And then the confusion would begin with the boats darting about like straws in the wind.

Rifles, Bren guns, mortars, ammunition, picks and shovels all had to have their place. With these and our packs and other stores – wireless sets, telephone cable and so on – there seemed barely an inch of freeboard even on this placid stretch of lake. The Brigade Staff were, I think, beginning to have grave doubts about our chances on the fast-flowing Irrawaddy in the dead of night. Even we ourselves, trusting though we were of our superiors, had begun to mutter our misgivings to one another.

In the event, however, a quantity of outboard motors were

brought up from somewhere. Pairs of canvas boats were lashed together with bamboo stauncheons and the outboards fastened between, thus giving more stability and control. Notwithstanding these innovations, the assault-crossing of the Irrawaddy was obviously going to be a matchstick and bootlace affair. The whole concept was quite anachronistic when one considered the Jap divisions, waiting for us on the other side of the river.

We began to take stock of our surroundings.

What a wonderful country this was . . . Here in the plains the trees were rounded and in varying shades of green. Crops of millet, rye and wild tomatoes grew in profusion. But the land was so dry that, where there was any movement, a thick rosy haze of powdery dust filled the air. For twelve hours every day the brassy sun hung in a cloudless blue sky, but by comparison with the mountainous jungle country further north the heat was dry and healthy.

Interspersed about the plain, trees grew in clumps. Spiky hedges and cacti interlaced the network of paddyfields around small wooded villages. Almost every village hereabouts is in a wood; the white pagodas, with their golden umbrellas shining in the sun, stand out above the palm fronds as the only sign of habitation. There are no roads; only well-worn switchback bullock-tracks between villages. It is an incredibly peaceful scene.

Unfortunately then, hidden silently away amongst all that beauty and serenity and divided only by the massive snaking river, lay the opposing armies of east and west.

South of Kandaw Tank, the great Irrawaddy river runs from east to west about eight miles distant. It is almost a mile wide in places and rarely less than a thousand yards; it has come down out of the eternal snows of the Himalayas, looping westwards at Mandalay and sweeping on again past Sagaing, Ngazun and the mouth of the Mu river. Immediately south and forty miles west of Mandalay, it washes the sandy edges of Myinmu, Wetto and Satpangon. Ten miles further west begins the gigantic southern loop towards Rangoon and the sea.

From the north, on a front of fifty miles, the divisions of the Fourteenth Army were converging rapidly onto this central area for what, it was hoped, would be the decisive battle of the war in Burma.

So there we were – in Kandaw, swimming in the murky brown waters of the tank and playing with our boats.

I wrote to my mother and brother in an attempt to console them, telling them that I was well out of danger and that my work kept me well away from the front. Emotionally my reactions seemed atrophied, although there were moments when waves of grief swept over me as I realised that never again would I know the quiet reassurance of my father's presence. Desperately I searched for the right words. It was hopeless. The other men were having similar difficulties with their own compositions; we were too far away, too separated by time, distance and events to make much real difference to our families. So long as each felt the other was safe and well, somewhere – there was hope. Life might one day be the same again as it once had been. We dared not contemplate anything else.

Physically the time at Kandaw could have been a very restful period despite the boat training.

But for some of us it was not to be.

Several patrols were sent across the Irrawaddy on reconnaissance. One of these led by Sergeants Hallwood and Robinson roamed the south bank amongst the enemy for five days, although they had rations for only three. They penetrated six miles south of the river and brought back a wealth of information.

Charlie Bates had been across even before the Satpangon battles. On that occasion when returning the boat had capsized half way and the patrol had to swim for it ending up amongst some Jap positions on the north bank. Their spectacular adventures before rejoining the Battalion would, I am sure, make better reading. My own experience of this kind of thing was, I am glad to say, insignificant by comparison but may give some idea of it.

TEN

Irrawaddy Patrol

"Brigade wants an officer patrol to go over the river, Coop."

Peter Clark, now officially in command of 'B' Company, settled himself comfortably in front of my bivouac of leaves and boughs a few feet from my platoon headquarters trench. The blood drained out of my face and I could hear my heart beating like a loose triphammer, as I answered nonchalantly enough.

"Oh, hard luck, Pete old chap! I'll see that things are kept in order for you here."

"Not me, you poor mutt, you – you're to cut along to Brigade for briefing right away."

Peter's phrase, 'patrol over the river', was terrifying enough. Getting over that bloody great sweep of water would be a major adventure in itself. But, once there, in the middle of the whole Japanese bloody army . . .

The Brigade Major briefed me himself over an excellent lunch of fried bully beef in the Pongyi Kyaung – a large one-storey wooden building which, until Brigade Headquarters had taken it over as an office, had been a combined school and Buddhist monastery.

The Brigadier himself spoke to me before my departure and I thought at one point that his use of my first name held an ominous ring. The informality suited my ego nevertheless, I suppose: had I not myself learned to use similar little tricks in my dealings with my own subordinates at times like these? I could hardly blame the old boy. He was fierce and fatherly, and by the time he had finished speaking to me, I was prepared to have just one more 'go' for this somewhat terrifying man.

When I returned to Battalion, I found that Colonel Harvey had been evacuated and that Peter Gillam had assumed command. He had personally called for volunteers for my patrol, no doubt using the same sort of tactics the Brigadier had used with me. Unfortunately his remark to the effect that all nine men were very strong swimmers left me in no doubt as to his unspoken misgivings. We were to use a couple of inflatable rubber recce-boats for the job.

Corporal Butterworth, from my own platoon, was the NCO in charge of one of the boats. The other eight men were from different companies, except for Ginger Lacey, Billy Orr and my platoon runner, Ernie Morrisroe; Taylor, one of the Battalion HQ intelligence section, was also in the party. I chose the four of them to make up the compliment of my own crew.

They assembled in my platoon area and I read their thoughts.

"All right, I know how you feel. You all know what this kind of patrol means. This is the form. We go to Myinmu in transport with the recce-boats. When it gets dark, a couple of Navy frogmen are going to swim across the Irrawaddy and place markers out for us on the far bank. The markers will be set up about two miles downstream on the far shore to allow for the current carrying us. It means paddling like hell if we're to get anywhere near them. The idea is to test the speed of the current and get timings to assist the staff in making their plans for the big crossing. That's the first part. Next, having hidden the boats, five of you stay put. The remainder strike out from the markers and recce the bridgehead area which is initially reckoned to be five hundred yards wide and about a quarter of a mile inland. That will be the job for my crew, Corporal Butterworth. If we are not back at the markers inside three hours, your job is to get back here and make your report about the strength of the current without delay. All clear? Any questions? Right, get your heads down for a couple of hours, leave all personal stuff with your platoon sergeants. The dress will be: canvas shoes, puttees, and Stens and grenades only. RV back here at 1600 hours, after grub."

At a few minutes after four o'clock in the afternoon we piled aboard a Dodge 10-hundredweight truck, onto which the rubber boats and paddles had already been loaded. My old friend, the Mule Transport Officer, was at the wheel with his batman alongside him. I think he was still smarting at my loss of the jeep in the Chindwin river. Leaning down from the cab with a dreadful leer, he said:

"Every time I see you there's trouble! Come on, we haven't much time – I want to be back here before stand-to. Don't fancy driving back in the dark. You and your bloody gang can play silly buggers as much as you like, after that."

About an hour later we were taken into a hut on the water's edge amongst the trees surrounding Myinmu. The place was familiar, having been part of 'B' Company's area when we had occupied the place earlier before the fight for Satpangon.

The front of the hut looked out across the vast expanse of water towards the enemy shoreline. It had an upper floor and was of course built of bamboo. These bashas are made of tubular bamboo for the framework and floors, and matting or hurdles for the walls. There were openings for windows. It was built on high stilts, and a shaky ladder led to the upper floor, which was just a box-like room with a peep-hole facing the river in one wall. In front of the peep-hole stood a matting-covered table, on which the standing patrol in charge of the place had set up a telescope. Beside this was a log-book. Pinned to the wall was a range-card showing distances to various reference points on the south side of the river. We spent the remaining hour or so of daylight in final briefing. Time and again I searched apprehensively with the telescope for enemy movement.

About an hour after dark a dozen shells sailed over our hiding-place and landed with a crump in the rear of the village. I had a water bottle half full of issue rum, which I passed round with some cigarettes rather solemnly.

"Right, lads: last smoke." I didn't intend emphasis on the word 'last'.

Shortly afterwards we bade farewell to the garrison in Myinmu and carried the rubber boats, already inflated, down to the water's edge, our faces and hands blackened like a party of nigger minstrels.

The moon rode high and brilliant, as only a Burma moon can; but mercifully for our peace of mind, there were huge banks of cloud. Out there we could still see the faint, dark outline of trees on the enemy side; but they blended into the blue-black sky, so that no features of the shore were distinguishable. Now and then, for long-minutes, great shadows crossed the land. Then only the stars cast their light over the calm, massive river.

A party of Indian soldiers, mostly Punjabis were supposed to meet us at this point. Their job was to cross just ahead of us and raid a Jap Observation Post a mile or so further downstream from the proposed bridgehead. The whole idea seemed a bit stupid to me, especially if one wished to maintain as much of the element of surprise as possible, when the operation was finally mounted and the Division put across. I had met the Indian patrol leader at the Brigadier's briefing session. He was a tall, handsome Pathan with pale skin, blue eyes and a cultured English accent. Presently he arrived with his men. They floundered about in the crackling broad leaves of maize where we were waiting. Corporal Butterworth and my men helped them out, when it became obvious that few had any idea how to use their Mae West life-belts. They tugged and pulled at the securing cords and blew furiously down the rubber tubes fixed to the valves. When finally the Indians had finished contorting themselves into the ungainly jackets, we settled down to wait for the frogmen to arrive.

When they did, they looked like men from another planet in their tight-fitting rubber suits and helmets. Apparently they had swum the Irrawaddy twice before in the last few days, and they both looked very calm and casual as they tugged on their gigantic flippers and adjusted the various bits of equipment with which their bodies were festooned. The taller of the two was a veritable Tarzan of a man. He explained to the Pathan captain and me that the markers they were carrying were, in fact, some sort of Aldis lamp, the light from which was cunningly shielded from every point except that at which the lamp was pointed. So we would need to keep a sharp look-out. They were prepared to remain on the far side as long as it took us to reach them. With that these fantastic men flip-flopped across the sand and disappeared like slippery monsters into the inky depths.

For what seemed like an age afterwards, as the moon rose higher in the sky, we gazed anxiously across the river. The Indian troops seemed edgy and ill at ease. Their tall commander kept up a constant nervous whispering with his Sergeant in Urdu. Sometimes he would address me in his remarkably fluent Oxford accent.

Eventually from miles away down river a faint orange light appeared, flickered once or twice and then held steady. At last the Navy men had arrived on the enemy side and, so it would appear, unmolested. I conferred with the Pathan. Suddenly he became quite agitated. He thought there was still far too much light for crossing, and he was not prepared to risk his large patrol in what he described as "this brutal moonlight". It was obvious to Butterworth and me that the fellow had a bad attack of wind-up. What was infinitely worse, his constant jabberings had transmitted his own anxiety and misgiving to practically every man in his patrol.

I argued that the orders were clear and that he should cross immediately the markers were in position. I can sound very fierce and aggressive when the occasion demands: but even my most severe attempt at histrionics held less terror for the lad than the fears built up in his imagination during the long wait for action. It seemed unreasonable to keep the frogmen waiting any longer: it was obvious that nothing short of shanghai-ing the Pathan and his patrol would suffice to get them moving that night.

I ordered my men into the dinghies. Scrambling aboard, lurching and floundering, we grabbed our paddles. The last man of each crew held us close-hauled while we settled down. Glancing back up the bank I could see the Indian patrol, sharply outlined against the sky, making off in a disorderly pack towards Myinmu dragging their boats with them.

I shouted something suitably scathing after the retreating back of the Pathan. But he made no answer, and then came a muffled oath from Butterworth's direction.

"Bloody hell! We're sinking."

This turn of events was the last straw. I jumped for firm ground with the anchor line in my hand. A fraction later we would have been hurtling away in the current.

The scene in the other dinghy might have been hilarious in any other situation. Butterworth, hanging on to the line, needed all his strength to hold the boat against the current, even close to shore.

"Somebody's shoved a bayonet or something through the bottom of the bugger," he cursed. "Out! Out, you sods, before I let you bloody well go."

The four members of his crew sat as though rooted to the dinghy, which was all but submerged.

"It wasn't me, sir", they at last managed almost in unison.

God! What a shambles, I thought.

"Right! Get the hell out of it. Put the boat in the maize and wait for us in Myinmu until first light, Corporal. If we're not back then, go home and tell the CO the whole story."

I climbed back into my own boat and Ernie Morrisroe shoved off. Ginger, the ex-Barnado's boy, muttered:

"For what we are about to receive . . ."

Then we were whirled away into the blackness and the unknown.

The Irrawaddy is silent and unruffled: one is totally unprepared for its terrible swiftness. I have always been a strong swimmer, but confronted now with crossing this living sea of dark water in our flimsy rubber dinghy, I was more than thankful for the Mae West life-belts.

It was extremely difficult to keep the boat pointing in the right direction. The men paddled like galley-slaves, but I think my job with the steering oar was even more strenuous than theirs. I thought we might all fail through sheer exhaustion before we got anywhere near the other side. I gave the order to paddle less furiously. The orange marker-light had disappeared the moment we got afloat and I gave up all idea of ever seeing it again. There were no landmarks visible as the banks of clouds had built up across the whole sky. We seemed to be swirling in a pitch black void, only aware of our direction by the pull of the current and our own weight balance in the boat.

I thought then that any attempt to send a large assault party over in this manner would spell utter disaster. It occurred to me that if the Indian patrol had tried it, as it had been expected to do, it would have been unlikely to have got very far as an organised unit.

I could not tell, now, how far out from Myinmu we were, nor how fast we were sweeping downstream. Ernie spoke against the splash of paddles and the stiff breeze over the water:

"Christ ! We could end up in bloody Rangoon!"

At that moment we felt utterly lost on a black sea. I looked at the luminous face of my watch, almost losing my grip on the steering oar as I did so. We had been afloat only thirty minutes: it seemed like hours. Suddenly I made out a whitish strip. The others had seen it too. We paddled like maniacs. As I strained my eyes, a gently shelving sandbank came into view. Seconds later we disembarked in indecent haste, wet through to the skin and shivering with cold and the strain of paddling. When we pulled the dinghy up the sand-bar it was half full of Irrawaddy water. We lay down to regain our breath. Presently Billy Orr spotted the orange marker. As the moon broke through a crack in the clouds it was possible to make

out the true bank of the river a hundred yards away across the intervening shallows. I sent Billy and Ginger to contact the frogmen.
Ernie, Taylor and I dragged the dinghy as quietly as we could the
rest of the way towards the steeply shelving bank, where we began
the job of hiding it in the undergrowth on top.

Presently the other two re-appeared with the frogmen. Apparently nothing untoward had happened since thay had arrived. I told
them to forget about waiting for the Indian patrol and they prepared to depart. The Tarzan character assured me that this bit of
beach was almost exactly at the the eastern end of the proposed
bridgehead. I gathered his calculations were made on a survey of
the known sand-bars, the largest of which we had struck as our first
landfall. Wishing us *bon voyage* for the return trip, the frogmen then
slithered down the bank and disappeared into the river as silently as
two giant fish, leaving us alone with the night.

There was a track leading through the scrub along the top of the
river bank. We followed it for about a hundred paces eastwards.
Slowly we progressed, warily, Sten guns ready, eyes shifting left,
right. The track opened out into a sandy clearing and we skirted
this, keeping in the shadow of the elephant grass which grew man-
high around it. It was much lighter now and the moon appeared
more frequently through the clouds. Carefully we edged round until
the whole clearing was behind us. We then found ourselves on the
top of a steep bank of shelving sand which ran down into a chaung.
To our left we could hear the lapping of water and see the steely
glint of the mighty river. Immediately to our right the dry chaung
led away into the scrub, and we moved silently along in the soft
sand below the lip of its near bank.

Each inch seemed a mile, each second an age, as we went on and
on. Every step might be mined. The chaung stretched away empty,
wide and menacing. Our progress was painfully slow, but we dared
not hurry. As we moved further inland, the sense of aloneness and
chilling fear gripped our stomachs. At last, after what we calculated
as five hundred paces, we climbed up the bank into the scrub and
began circling away from the chaung to the west. After a while we
discovered a narrow path, hard-packed and rutted as though by
bullock carts. It was getting easier to see and stars began to appear
through the clouds, lighting the way like lanterns hanging in
bunches in the sky. The westward reconnaissance took almost an

hour: we were moving a foot at a time, carefully, patiently. Suddenly the earth vibrated and we froze stiffly, paralysed. A bright searching flash split the night, followed by the sound of shells wobbling and skittering through the air above. We fell flat. Away across the river to our right the shells hit, and muffled explosions carried back to us across the expanse of water and scrub.

We lay listening, while salvo after salvo screamed and whimpered overhead. I signalled the others and we went on our way, wheeling away from the bullock track back towards the river. We felt more confident somehow; the worst seemed over. I prayed silently:

"Jesus, don't let any of us become careless now."

The patrol had seemed endless, but at last we found the track above the river bank and followed it back eastwards parallel with the Irrawaddy. We knew with an unerring sixth sense when we neared the dried-up river bed once more. Somewhere in the grass and bushes was the dinghy. We slid to the ground, automatically observing all around.

A cool breeze dried the sweat on us and we could hear the faint sound of our breathing, magnified like all sounds in the night.

I glanced at my watch: the patrol had taken us exactly three hours. Across the track the trees stood mute on the edge of the clearing and I looked away to one side: if one stared too long, things began to move. No one spoke, no one had spoken for three hours. We were anxious to be away but not yet ready to brave the terrors of the river. I needed a cigarette badly. With the thought the familiar, sweet smell of tobacco smoke drifted on the air. Each one of us turned his head, as the message hit us instantaneously . . . Japs. Faces in the dust, hands clammily grasping our weapons and grenades, we pressed lower against the sheltering earth and waited. I was sure the pounding of my heart could be heard ten yards off.

"Don't let anybody cough. Please don't let them see us."

I repeated the silent prayer over and over as the prickly grass tickled my face. The scented dust in my nostrils brought an almost uncontrollable urge to sneeze.

Along the track came a line of ponies, each one led by a helmeted Jap soldier. They had short carbines slung across their backs. The pungent aroma of sweating horse flesh and the unmistakable smell of iodine came to us through the perfumed dust kicked up by the ponies' hooves. Snaffling and clinking, the whole party passed

within a few feet of where we lay and slithered down into the
chaung a dozen yards away. Then we heard something else – the
metallic double clack-clack of a rifle being cocked. A tall shirt-
sleeved Japanese towered over us on the track. The man seemed to
be looking down at us where we lay in the shadow of the scrub.
For an unbearable second or two I hovered on the brink of a
coronary . . . then the Jap moved on, away down into the chaung
after the others.

By crawling just a foot or two we could see down into the moon-
washed slash of sand below our hiding-place, across to where the
enemy party were splashing in the shallows of the Irrawaddy on the
near side of the sand-bar. They were filling up some sort of metal
containers with water. Some of the Japs were smoking. There was a
chattering unconcern about the whole operation which told me how
infinitely secure they must feel behind the vast water barrier of the
Irrawaddy river. There were about thirty of them and roughly the
same number of animals.

Everything seemed strangely unreal in an unreal world.

"God!" I thought, "What the hell are we all doing here? Those
scruffy, smelly creatures down there and us up here . . . in this
remote land."

The patrol had told on my nerves and I had the unreasonable
foolish urge to stand up and shout, or even to smash away at the
Japanese water party with Stens and grenades. The strain was
almost unbearable. When the hell would they move?

At last they went off inland, shuffling along in the chaung dust.
Some of them were singing and their high-pitched feminine laughter
could be heard long after they were out of sight. Rolling over on
our backs, we breathed in great gulps of air and gingerly eased our
limbs to bring back the circulation.

"Bloody hell!" whispered Ernie; "that was close – bloody hundreds of the little sods."

"I thought that bastard at the end of the line had seen us," was
Billy's rejoinder.

We made haste to find the dinghy and I almost had a fit when at
first we failed to locate it. Finally, after scrabbling around for a
minute or two, Ginger fell over the steering paddle and everyone
began to make far too much noise.

"For God's sake!" I whispered hoarsely; "we've been lucky so far, but we're not home yet. Stow it, for Christ's sake!"

We carried the dinghy across the shallows, splashing and gasp-ing, and launched it in the river. As we fell aboard like five drunks, the dinghy seemed to ship almost enough water to sink us. We ignored it and began to paddle like mad things for the home shore. Then I remembered the Mae West life jackets. We had left them all behind in the scrub . . .

At first the return trip was a far more tolerable experience than the outward one had been. We could make out the friendly shore-line when we were still quite far out, but the sense of speed with which we were being hurtled downstream was disconcerting. We had paddled hard at first but most of our strength and the sense of urgency was soon gone: it was with minimum of effort that any headway was attained. As the northern shore came closer, certain landmarks began to appear. Suddenly a faint silhouette which seemed familiar loomed up out of the velvety night: the pagodas of Wetto. Then the plantation. And then, unmistakably, the outline of Satpangon and the graveyard pagodas. We were eight miles down-stream from Myinmu and drifting ever further each passing minute.

"Pouff! Pouff!"

A bright golden light flooded the scene around us. Two flares hung spluttering above our heads and threw the ghostly silhouettes into relief . . . then two more. In an instant the realisation dawned upon me.

"Paddle – paddle like hell! It's the Gurks. They probably think we're Japs!"

Our arms suddenly felt leaden. As I strained my eyes towards the Gurkha positions in Satpangon, there were flashes near the water's edge and bullets whined somewhere overhead. A long burst of Bren-gun fire scarred the night, followed by rifle shots. Ginger slumped sideways and disappeared into the river without a sound.

Water poured into the dinghy and we lurched and spun round like a cork in a whirlpool. Billy lost his paddle and we almost cap-sized as he grabbed for it. Ernie was shouting something. Little silver spouts of water shot up as bullets cracked and zipped about us into the river. The next thing I remember was the four of us over the side, holding onto the gunwales of the dinghy, kicking and thrashing with our legs in an effort to take the boat in nearer to the shore.

The whole incident could not have lasted more than twenty or thirty seconds. By then we were well down stream, such was the strength of the inshore current.

Finally we staggered ashore and clambered up the steep bank. Satpangon was at least half a mile distant. Hurriedly we deflated the dinghy and left it hidden in some long grass. Then we moved away from the Irrawaddy: we had finished with that terrible river for the time being. Making a nest for ourselves amongst some tall elephant grass, we threw off our pouches and fell to the ground exhausted.

After a little while we began to feel hungry and searched around until we unearthed some soggy, hard-tack biscuits. Taylor found some Tiger Brand cigarettes and wax matches which had miraculously remained dry, owing to the strip of adhesive tape wrapped round the lid of his tobacco tin.

Quietly we chewed on the biscuits and drew on Taylor's fags, talking about Ginger. We cursed the staff for having failed to inform the Gurkhas in Satpangon about our patrol.

Just before dawn we were dozing, feeling snug and secure in our nest in the long grass. Only half conscious of the pale dawn filtering through the undergrowth, I sensed, rather than heard, movements around our hide. The animal reaction to approaching danger brought me suddenly to my feet in a swirling ground-mist. Immediately I was knocked flat again as a body hurtled against my back. There was a high-pitched scream from someone nearby and the sound of trampling feet in the dry tall grass. Momentarily the hide seemed to be filled with men and dust, and the sounds of stampede, together with the strange gurgling moans of a man in awful pain. At first I thought that I had experienced a fantastic nightmare. I was bathed in sweat and my limbs twitched uncontrollably. Gradually I focused my whirling senses.

Then I heard Billy's voice whispering hoarsely. I felt my way across the hide and found him leaning over someone in the tangled grass.

"What the hell's happened? Who is it?"

"It's Taylor," he answered. "They've bayoneted the poor bugger."

Taylor was on his face moaning, and the back of his shirt and trousers felt sticky with blood.

Number 6 Platoon

Sergeant 'Lakri' Woods

Private Jones, Private 'Jock' Lawson, Morrisroe (at rear, in forage cap), the author's batman, Private Smith (right)

Rafting down the Chindwin: C.S.M. Jim Walker (with wrist watch),
Sergeant 'Busty' O'Connor (bareheaded centre), and Private Billy Orr
(bareheaded, centre rear)

Major Alistair Falconer (cleaning his rifle) with Ted Moore and the author

Traffic control post on the Tamu Road

Midday halt

Company 'Cook-house'

The area covered by the patrol and the subsequent initial bridgehead

The burning village

Cemetery on Kohima Ridge:

When you go home
Tell them of us, and say
For your tomorrow
We gave our today

"Who bayoneted him?" I hissed. "Christ! Am I mad? What's happened?"

A voice croaked behind me. It was Ernie. He was swaying slightly against the wall of grass and I could barely recognise his strained features in the cold light.

"I thought they were Gurks from Satpangon. Taylor heard them too and shouted to them. But they were Japs – in here and out before you could spit."

After that I had time to look at Taylor. He was breathing noisily as I turned him over and his head flopped back. Then he seemed to stop breathing. For a minute he lay quiet and grey and then he began to mutter strange, soft moans as I held him. Billy and I somehow got our sodden field dressing on the stab wounds in his back.

Then I tried to make up my mind what to do next. The nearest help was in Satpangon and that was where we went eventually, somehow carrying Taylor along with us. I don't know how we managed it. We were all in, practically unconscious on our feet with exertion and the events of the past twelve hours. I had lost one of my canvas shoes in the river. As we approached the Satpangon perimeter, we shouted again and again. At last some Gurkhas came out, rifles at the ready, and relieved us of our burden.

Their medical officer looked us over and took the opportunity of lancing a lump on my right heel which oozed green pus: it was the size of an egg. Later we were taken by jeep to Brigade Headquarters, having first delivered Taylor to the Regimental Aid Post in Kandaw. He had four bayonet wounds in his back and legs. But he was smiling when the stretcher bearers carried him off:

"Biggest balls-up since the Somme!" he croaked at us as we said goodbye.

Then I found myself in the Pongyi Kyaung with the Brigade Major and his Intelligence Officer. On a table in front of me was a mug half full of rum. During the debriefing I kept falling off to sleep. At last they left me alone and I curled up in a corner of the room and slept like a dog.

ELEVEN

Myinmu Bridgehead

From an approximate total of three hundred and forty effectives in the four rifle companies before the Satpangon fight, the Company strengths were now reduced by almost forty per cent. Despite these heavy losses, with no apparent expectation of reinforcements, we were nevertheless chosen as the assault force for the Irrawaddy crossing.

The orders came from Brigade. As it happens I still have my original notes of them: scribbled in indelible pencil on the back of the last letter I ever received from my father, the words have run but they can just be deciphered. Here, in the full obscurity of military abbreviation, they are:

Infor.   Own Tps: 19 Div. 2 Div. 20 Div.
           Enmy: 31–33 Div. opposite.

Int.   100 Bde.   Establish BH.

Meth.   2 Border
          14 F.F.R.
          Bde. HQ.
          4/10 Gurkhas

Sup.   Complete Corps Arty.
          22 R.Es.
          Thunderbolts.
          268 Indep. Bde.
          Main landing by 17 Div. south of Monywa.

Rations – 2 days light scale
           1 days Compo

Coy. of M.M.Gs. to go over in last flight of boats.

Lamps put down by forward coys.
Two F.O.O. parties – one with each fwd. coy.
Bde. HQ will lay on underwater line which will connect up with N. bank.
Ammo. Riflemen carry 100 rounds
4 × 36 grenades 2 × 77 grenades
and 25 Bren mags per gun.
Tac. HQ at F.U.P. A.D.S. at Satpangon.

When first coy. crosses assembly area it will take with it its boats.
All stores, rations, etc. carried by fwd. coys. will be dumped and troops will move fwd. unimpeded.

We packed up and set off on the short but gruelling nine-miles march back to Satpangon. It was a strange feeling, lying up in the long grass outside the village again. Later I went inside to receive final orders and to be shown where the assault boats were hidden. On my way back to the platoon I passed the place where we had buried our dead after the attack and counted the small wooden crosses surmounting the shallow graves. There were fifty-three of them.

We lay for hours in the choking dust alongside a track behind the village, laden like Christmas trees, under packs, pouches, half-blankets, water bottles, Bren Magazines, grenades, rifles and all our other impedimenta.

Each company commander knew which flight his company was in, when it would cross, and where it would go when it reached the other side. Each platoon leader knew, or had a good idea, of the whole plan. Every man knew his place in the boats and where to go on landing. The operation had been planned down to the smallest detail of preparation and timing.

A procession of people came and went, shuffling and whispering along the track past our hide – artillery officers and their teams of signallers, engineers, mortarmen and machine-gunners humping their terrible loads.

It was nearly time to go, to start out once more down that long, long road to Rangoon and Singapore, where sixty thousand of our comrades, prisoners of war, were waiting for us to come and set them free.

The moon made shadows on the wall of trees behind us, the eerie shuffle of the footfall of silent men went on and on down the lane of white guide tapes. The ghostly outline of the shattered village of Satpangon cast its spell of treachery, fear and evil over those of us who knew and would never forget its terror.

It was hoped to make a surprise crossing unsupported by artillery; but the sound of outboard motors would obviously alert any Japanese in the vicinity. To overcome this, to some extent, it was left to a cab-rank of Anson aircraft to fly low up and down the river to mask the noises of our approach . . . God bless the gilded staff!

'A' and 'D' companies were to go in the first flight and then form the south and west sides of the bridgehead respectively. 'B' company was to cross third and fill in the eastern side along the bank of the chaung, where we had watched the Jap water party on my recent ill-fated patrol.

At last the order came to move. We made our way along the tapes to where the boats were concealed a hundred yards or so from the water's edge.

The crews sorted themselves out. As we lifted the boats and began to shamble forward, the first outboards exploded into life as the leading wave took off.

"God Almighty, what a bloody racket!" said Peter Clark who was lurching and sweating with the boat next to mine. "That will most certainly have awakened Marshal Kimura and Tojo as well, without a doubt."

The comments from the men included the favourite Battalion catch-phrase:

"Biggest balls-up since the Somme!"

We stared into the night and cursed the Anson crews, who were at that precise moment swanning up and down above the river about ten miles away in the direction of Myinmu.

"We're damned lucky we're not in the first wave anyway", said Dick.

"Shut up," whispered Jock. "Save your blatherin' and put some muscle behind this bloody boat!"

Muffled curses and the clank and bump of weapons and equipment against the wood and canvas sides of the boat accompanied us the rest of the way to the water.

Our turn came and we piled aboard, as we had practised so often in the Kandaw Tank. The outboards rasped out and away we swirled – a small armada of antiquated boats, a couple of hundred frightened men floating, ever so slowly, in the dead of night across one of the greatest rivers in Asia.

Kimura's hordes must have been trembling in their bunkers! The whole set-up was fantastic. But at the half-way mark it still seemed somehow feasible. So we held to our course, staring anxiously ahead.

About three-quarters of the way across we saw some rubber boats going around in circles. These were some of 'D' Company's craft – dinghies tied in groups of three behind the wood and canvas assault boats, which were towing them along. In the strong current, the rubber dinghies must have become difficult to control. Some of them had swung round into a figure S, and one or two had already broken away and were being swept downstream, entangling the towlines and outboard motors.

Soon after this, as if to confirm our earlier misgivings, several bursts of light-machine-gun fire slashed the night with orange-coloured tracer above our heads. The whole business was rapidly becoming decidedly unpleasant when my own boat hit the bank. Everyone jumped out at once, despite my shouts for an orderly disembarkation. One of the men became inextricably entangled in his equipment in five feet of rushing water and was carried away immediately, threshing in the current. We never saw him again.

The beach seemed deserted. We made our way to the top of the bank through the sand dunes and waited a minute or two until the other three boats, with my sections aboard, beached behind us. Sergeant Woods gathered the men round him and led off at the head of a single file towards the chaung. I left Ernie Morrisroe to guide Peter and the rest of the Company ashore if and when they arrived. In the moonlight the chaung looked like the bone-white skeleton of a fish, as we took up a hasty all-round defence on top of the bank overlooking the river. Soon Ernie arrived with the others and Peter allocated platoon positions amongst the sandy hillocks and scrub. While we dug ourselves in, a Jap machine-gun, hidden in the undergrowth on the opposite bank of the chaung some three hundred yards away, fired at the noises coming from the direction of the crossing. Later there was some more firing to our right where 'A' Company were supposed to be.

At about five in the morning, with the moon full up, a Jap patrol came down the chaung, strung out in full view and strolling along quite casually. My right-hand section let them come in close and then grenaded them. The Japs beat it back up the chaung as fast as they could go, leaving two of their number lying in the sand. Within minutes there came the soft plop-plop of the enemy knee-mortars and the roar of the exploding bombs amongst the scrub. But by then we were all well and truly below ground in the sand dunes.

Battalion signallers got a telephone cable through to us. An ammunition party came up with RSM Pope, who told us that the four rifle companies were all in position, with Battalion HQ established in the scrub about three hundred yards down the track behind us.

The night wore on without further incident. We began to relax and thank providence for the ease with which we had got ourselves over the river and established the embryo bridgehead.

As we stood to at dawn, the two Jap 'bodies' in the chaung suddenly climbed to their feet, slouched into a narrow ravine and disappeared out of sight.

"Cheeky bastards!" said Dick. "If they're going to treat this business as bloody casually as that, you can bet your boots we're up against a right handy bunch."

The field telephone rasped in its tin container.

"Something's up, I bet," said Dick again. He had assumed temporary duties once more as CSM, and I was at the Company command post with him while Peter was doing his rounds of the platoon positions.

It was Peter Gillam, the Acting Commanding Officer, on the line. Somehow, as always, he re-instilled a sense of urgency into the proceedings.

"The Gurkhas are coming over in an hour," he told me. "By the time they get here I want 'B' Company on the other side of that chaung of yours, and then we're all going to squash over to the left so that Johnny Gurk can take up positions on our right. Clear?" he added.

"Yes, Sir."

"Then tell Clark I shall expect you in the new position by 0700. Out."

I passed this on to Peter when he returned. He gave hurried orders and led us out onto the flat chaung as the sun came over the horizon beyond Mandalay.

For some reason he led at a tangent towards the water's edge, instead of directly at the opposite bank of the chaung. Instinctively I knew he was as aware of hidden eyes watching us as I was myself. When the whole Company was dotted out in extended formation across the mouth of the delta and almost exactly mid-way between our recently vacated trenches and the hummocks and sand hills on the farther bank of the three-hundred-yard wide chaung . . . then and only then, as though on some unrealistically planned exercise, did the enemy divulge his presence.

Not one man with whom I spoke of the incident later expected anything else from the moment we had stood up and walked uncomplainingly into the jaws of an ambush.

When the tracer bullets came hissing out of the scrub, stitching patterns in the sand around our feet, it was as if to awaken us all from some ghastly somnambulistic walk; as though, until that moment, we had been spectators of our fate in a nightmare sequence, the reality of which could not penetrate until shattered by the noise of the cracking shot about us.

The machine-guns were still too far away to rush. It was the hell of a long run back to the trenches. Our one hope was the Irrawaddy. The nearest men to the river were already in it. In seconds we hit the wet sand, scratching at it with our fingernails. In the shallows there was a slight depression where the water had shelved away at the shoreline. Flat on our bellies in the swirling current we lay hypnotised, hardly daring to move, waiting for the bullets which would slam into our helmets.

The bewildering, numbing sensation of fear and panic held all of us, until the men at the end of the line, nearest the trenches got up and began to run. Tracer bullets sped and slammed into the back and legs of one of them, fizzling in the sodden pack as his body rolled back under the water. The others splashed back into the river, crawling, horrified. The last man collapsed with three yards to go, hit in the thigh. Two others dragged him by the pack straps after them, leaving him face down in the water as another burst splattered into the sand.

All this happened inside thirty seconds and before anyone had gathered his wits sufficiently to do anything but try to save his own skin.

Then Sergeant Woods threw a smoke grenade, and then another.

A Bren team, taking advantage of the temporary cover afforded by the smoke, got their gun into action. But it was a hopeless business. The Japs had the advantage of the rising sun directly behind them. We could barely make out the white ridge of sand and scrub in which their guns were hidden. More phosphorous grenades were flung out: as they burst I somehow gathered myself together and ran for the nearest mortarman. He was loath to move and I didn't blame him. Between us we fired off half a dozen 2-inch smoke bombs and by that time the Company Commander and a few NCOs had rallied the men sufficiently to get them moving back towards the trenches. But it was a stampede as the smoke receded. Packs, weapons, picks, shovels, cases of bombs, all lay in discarded heaps in the path of our mad flight for cover.

Undoubtedly those smoke grenades and the 2-inch mortar smoke bombs saved us from an unholy battering, as they had so often before. It was not until we fell back into our so recently vacated trenches on top of the river bank that we first became aware of new and much more potent help. From somewhere across the Irrawaddy Vickers machine-guns were firing long bursts over our heads, and heavy mortar bombs were crumping into the scrub around the Japanese position.

It was then that we saw a figure, still fifty yards away, up to his waist in the shallows and struggling towards us with another man across his shoulders. It was my Sergeant Woods. Someone called for rapid fire to cover them.

Slowly, as Lakri drew nearer, we became aware of the almost superhuman effort he was making to retain his feet in the dragging current. The wounded man sagged like a heavy sack across his back. As Woods heaved himself towards the steep shelving bank, a couple of us ran down to help. Before we were half way down the dune, a fresh burst of enemy fire drubbed into the sand round the struggling man. Lakri spun like a top. Clutching at tufts of grass he rolled and cartwheeled back down the slope into the river. His face and the upper part of his body were covered in his own blood and that of the man he had been carrying. Almost immediately he was back on his feet, knee-deep in the river. Then he began to run around the sheltering dune and disappeared from our view. The wounded man was left spreadeagled below us on the bank.

The Company stretcher-bearer, Wilcox, who had run forward

with me, was groaning with pain. He held his left hand tightly under his right armpit and blood was dripping onto the sand as he lay beside me.

"We'll run down and drag him by the legs into the river," I shouted. "Can you give me a hand?"

"One fukkin' hand's all I've got," Wilcox replied. "Go on, you give the word. I'm with you."

I went over the edge of the dune in a slithering crouch with Wilcox beside me. We each grabbed a leg of the wounded man, as we reached him, and without pause continued our wild slide towards the lapping water below. While we struggled the few feet round the bank to safety, another Jap burst thudded into the sand and a bullet slapped into the wounded man's chest. Black blood oozed from his nostrils and mouth, and great moans and sighs came from him as he fought for breath. We saw then that it was Reid, Peter Clark's batman. How we got him the two hundred yards along the river bank to the RAP. I'll never know. Lakri was already there and I waited until he was put aboard a ferrying DUKW, together with Reid and Wilcox.

Lakri had a bullet through one arm but appeared as stoical as ever.

"Wish the lads good luck from me, Skipper. I'll be back as soon as I can."

His voice came as though from a great distance. I raised my hand in salute.

"Biggest balls-up since the Somme," I managed, and Lakri gave me two fingers in reply.

Slowly I walked back to the Company position in a numbing haze of shock.

TWELVE

"Stand Fast 'B' Company"

I found Peter lying at the bottom of his command post, a blood-soaked handkerchief wrapped around one wrist. He was quite obviously badly shocked and his Headquarters men were trying to persuade him to go back to the Aid Post.

"No," I heard Peter shouting his face twisted in an agonised expression. "No! No! No! Bloody no!"

I plunged into the hole beside him, conscious only of the desire to get my head below ground. There were still men running backwards and forwards trying to find cover, and it was all too obvious that the Company was in a state of utter confusion after the appalling shock of the ambush. I felt as if I had run a fast quarter mile and the breath was tearing at my lungs. All around me I could hear the gasping, breathless curses of men and the crack of tracer bullets criss-crossing little more than feet above the grass stalks on the edge of the trench.

Eventually things began to quieten down and I told Peter that I would bandage his wound properly. There was a neat blue-black blood-congealed hole drilled through his wrist: it must have been causing him intense pain now that the initial shock was wearing off. But he never murmured, and his concern was all for the other wounded and the bodies of four of his men which we could see near the water's edge two hundred yards away on the beach. Numerous rifles, packs, and piles of equipment, as well as three Bren guns, discarded in the stampede of our wild flight, lay out there also – grim reminders and evidence of the mad panic. Our escape had been little short of miraculous. Had it not been for the fortuitous crash-action support given us by our unknown saviours on the other side of the Irrawaddy, the Company would doubtless have been cut to pieces. Those

Japanese across the way had experienced a machine-gunner's dream.

Later on Peter was called to Battalion HQ for orders. I felt desperately sorry for him as he crawled away with his runner to the rear. How, if at all, he would explain the debacle on the beach and our failure to exploit this sector of the bridgehead further in all these hours, I could not imagine. Before he returned Dick Florence and I found ourselves plenty to do attempting to reorganise the demoralised Company. This was damned difficult, as even some of the NCOs had turned 'bolshie' and were threatening to soldier no more if we couldn't handle them better than we had that morning. When Peter returned and told us that the CO had insisted on us making another attempt to cross the chaung, the NCOs refused point-blank and stalked off back to their sections and platoons. It took all our powers of persuasion, while constantly toing and froing between groups of men all along the line, before we convinced them that, with artillery support and the cover of darkness, we could make it.

Some time during the afternoon RSM Pope brought forward an ammunition party, loaded down with hand grenades, and we spent the remaining hours of daylight fusing these and alternately smoking and dozing in our crumbling slit-trenches.

At eight o'clock the gunners brought down a concentrated barrage of high explosive onto the Jap positions, and under cover of this we led the anxious Company down onto the chaung and stalked forward in a disorderly mob towards the distant bank.

Almost before the barrage subsided we were climbing the dunes and ferreting amongst the long grass, where we found the mangled corpses of a few Japanese, together with an array of weapons, equipment, discarded mess tins, and the remains of two smashed machine-guns on tripods. Of most interest was a leather map-case: in it were beautifully executed crayon-drawings of pagodas and the Irrawaddy, together with military panoramas serving as range-cards. Peter made a rapid survey of the area and allotted platoon positions in the form of an all-round triangular defence.

My platoon took post on the Irrawaddy side; Busty O'Connor, who had been given Peggy O'Neil's platoon, dug in along the chaung bank in the rear; Paddy Castle's men filled in the longer side facing inland and eastwards. While we were digging, standing patrols from Paddy's platoon covered us as we worked.

Dick and I dug a trench together and congratulated ourselves on the ease with which we had got across the chaung. The chink-chink of digging and whispered conversation went on for some time until everyone had a place below ground. Then I went to confer with Peter: he was helping his signallers to put the finishing touches to his command-post trench in the centre of the perimeter amongst the soft sand and trampled elephant grass.

We talked for a minute or two in low tones. He sat on the edge of his hole with his water bottle held in his good hand, his left arm slung inside his web equipment. He took a swig from the bottle and then offered it to me. It was obvious that Peter had been dosing himself with rum: I could smell it on his breath. It rumbled in his empty stomach and he belched softly.

"You had better come in here with me, Coop. We'll relieve each other on watch," he said.

Something made me decline the invitation. I pointed out that we were the only officers in the Company: it would be as well to keep separate, in order to lessen the risk of both of us being knocked off at the same time. Peter thought about that. He then suggested that I attach the end of a length of copper wire to my wrist, so that he could communicate with me during the night – two tugs for my turn on duty; three tugs would signify that he wanted me at the command post. At first I thought he was joking. He was quite serious, however, and to humour him I agreed. I returned to my own slit-trench trailing the wire irritably.

Dick Florence sensed my irritation and I told him I would walk round the perimeter for a bit. The standing patrols were brought in and everyone seemed fairly well settled, with weapons ready and grenades stock-piled on the lip of the trench parapets. As the men answered my whispered queries, I sensed that their confidence was returning. Our quick walk over the chaung behind the barrage had done wonders in helping to restore morale. It must have been around midnight when I got back to my own trench. Dick started to say something, but his words were lost in a welter of noise and smoke, and heat and fear. Bombs and grenades dropped in amongst us thick and fast. And cries and screams made a shrill shambles of the night.

The grass caught fire and men staggered choking from the slit-trenches. Some fired at their friends, not knowing them in the flaming confusion.

Back through the flames and explosions some of Paddy's platoon came running, eyes peering wildly out of blackened faces. Better to run out into the open sand in the chaung behind our perimeter, than stay and die in the blinding noise with Japanese apparently everywhere. The place seemed crowded with men in the brief moments that these events registered on my bemused senses.

The grenades bursting made my ears sing and my head ache with the thunderous row. Men were flopping and rising, crawling and blundering their way about like maddened cattle in a barn-fire.

"Stand fast, 'B' Company. Stay where you are. Anyone that moves is a Jap."

Peter's voice was like a whiplash, bringing sanity and order into the boiling whirlpool of our panic-stricken and confused senses.

I popped my head up out of the trench into which I had thrown myself at the first explosion. There was a fearful bang like a cannon shot nearby, and I fell back against Dick as though poleaxed.

In the next trench were a skinny lance-corporal named Taylor and his mate Brady. Streams of curses were coming from them. As I regained my feet, I heard Taylor crying above the bursting grenades:

"My eye, my eye . . . I've lost my bloody eye."

Fighting back a numbing fear, I snaked over the lip of the parapet and slid into his trench.

"Quiet, for God's sake, quiet," I hissed. "You'll have the bastards in here if you don't keep quiet."

A Jap grenade had actually exploded in the trench between them. In some inexplicable way it had left Brady untouched, except by blast, but Taylor's screams left me in no doubt about his fate. A round black object dangled below the eye socket on his left cheek.

"It's me eye, sir," he groaned. "Me bloody eye's out."

As if the sequel to this remark was quite natural, he dragged his field-dressing out and with difficulty opened the wrapping. Holding his head in a queer sideways manner like a man with a deformed neck, he allowed the eyeball to rest on the dressing pad. Then he threw back his head and squeezed the eye back into its socket. I leaned across and shakily secured the ends of the bandage and replaced his steel helmet on his head.

"Don't worry. I'll have you out of this as fast as I can. Keep down and try not to make a noise."

My morphine tablets in their small glass phial had somehow gone adrift and I could not relieve him when the pain came. I took my water bottle and washed some of the blood from his face. As I did so, he stroked the back of my hand gently and kept repeating:

"I'll be OK, I'll be OK."

When I could I scrambled back to my own trench. The Japs were by now all round our small perimeter. They were out on the sand of the river bank and the chaung behind us, and we felt sure they were in some of Paddy's slit-trenches too. It was impossible to check on the situation properly. To move, even to the next trench, was a suicidal act, and Dick cursed me for having taken the risk once. It was against every rule of that lurid game. What the extent of the perimeter left to use was, we could only guess. We tried to judge from the sound of flying grenade-levers pinging in the air as they were released by our men.

We had to keep constantly alert with the alertness of cornered animals in the crowding darkness, and I felt mentally exhausted. It was impossible to tell if the enemy would eventually rush in amongst us, or whether even now they were creeping about silently in the long grass, murdering our men in their slit-trenches piece-meal.

Few, during that long night, fired a rifle or automatic weapon. Apart from the fact that an army standing order forbade the practice at night, unless one actually saw a Jap at point-blank range, it would merely have served to pin-point the exact position of a trench and make the enemy's task that much easier.

We just crouched in our holes and waited and prayed for the end of the night, and flung grenades in the direction of any sound we heard. At least the others did. Dick and I were roughly eight or ten yards behind what had been the outer defence of the perimeter above the Irrawaddy river bank. We dared not throw in case we hit our own men.

The grenade battle went on for fully six hours. Towards dawn we could tell that the enemy had pulled back a little way, as the soft plop-plop of his knee-mortars signified. These were catapult con-traptions which gave their grenades a much greater range than our own. The finale was rather a one-sided affair. There was an interval of perhaps two or three minutes between each salvo, and more than once the trench where Dick and I were was filled with smoke and dust and the acrid fumes of high explosive. The white flashes and ear-splitting crashes nearby almost drove us demented. At one point I found myself at the bottom of the trench with Dick slapping my face and cursing me under his breath. I think I must have fallen asleep – something to do with a psychological escape from a situation in which I could do nothing but endure. I forced myself upright, head low, standing my bayoneted rifle under my chin in case I dropped off again.

"Keep awake, sir. For Christ's sake, keep awake; it's bleedin' suicide if you drop down there," Dick hissed at me relentlessly.

During the night I had attached the end of the wire which Peter had given to me to my wrist. Eventually, tired of having my arm yanked skywards amongst the flying splinters of steel, I had taken off my pack and transferred the wire to one of the straps. As the sky came gradually lighter I noticed that my pack was now nowhere to be seen.

Then the Japs began to call out to us in English:

"Are you there, Johnny? Come out. Over here 'B' Company." It was all very eerie.

In thirty minutes it was full light. As the grey shafts of morning fell on the smoking grass and the hillocks of burnt stubble, we slowly crept from our 'funk-holes' in the sand and tentatively looked about us.

Twenty-three men had spent that fearful night together. Seven of those never saw the light of day. Several more, including the dauntless Lance-Corporal Taylor, were taken back across the chaung on stretchers, later in the morning.

We buried the dead on the dusty low cliff above the river, alongside the Japs we had found the previous evening, their shallow graves marked with wooden crosses made from grenade boxes.

In the late morning our 'deserters' were shepherded back to us across the chaung by RSM Pope, who also brought up more grenades. The men who had run away when the Japs had first attacked were very shamefaced. But we found it hard to condemn them and now they were back . . . what the hell did it matter anyway? The way things had been, it could have happened to anyone.

We found the corpse of a Japanese officer lying half in and half out of Brady's trench. Taylor swore to us, before he was carried away by the stretcher-bearers, that the Japs had tried to pull the body away, and that Brady had kept pulling it back again throughout half the night. When I asked him, Brady merely said:

"I got the sod and I wanted him!"

The Jap was a tall good-looking specimen, with creamy skin and cropped black hair growing low down his cheeks and neck. Lying beside him was his long two-handed Samurai sword.

Jock Lawson and Andie Thomas, who had shared a trench, had begun the night with thirty-six hand grenades each. By dawn they had been reduced to hurling clods of earth and stones at a group of Japs who had constantly approached and withdrawn, hour after hour. Jock looked haggard and edgy with exhaustion. He was busying himself tending to Andie, who had been slightly wounded early on. Nevertheless this tough Liverpool Welshman had continued to defend his trench and back up Jock throughout the night.

The RSM made scathing remarks about the lack of evidence of enemy casualties when Dick reported that we had used over four hundred grenades during the fight. If the Japs had only used the same number, it meant we had survived eight hundred ear-splitting explosions inside an area less than fifty yards square.

There was plenty of evidence, if you looked for it, however: the sand and grass all round the perimeter trenches was stained with blood and trails lead away into the scrub, where bodies had obviously been dragged. It would not have been like the Jap to leave any dead lying around, if he could help it.

Colour Sergeant Dickson brought two water paniers across the chaung to us at mid-day when we were nearly crazy with thirst in the baking dried-up scrub. The Irrawaddy was not far away across a flat expanse of dazzling white sand. But no one felt like a walk across that for water – we had been caught out there before!

I found my pack in Peter's command post. The signaller who had provided the copper wire was sitting beside the trench with a dirty bandage round his head under his earphones. Peter was cleaning his rifle. He looked up at me with a quizzical expression round his eyes. I glanced at my pack which still had the wire attached to it, and then back at Peter. Suddenly we both became convulsed with hysterical laughter.

The signaller waited until we had calmed down. Then with a

warm grin spreading across his dirt-streaked features, he said: quite deliberately, "You bloody daft couple of sods!"

THIRTEEN

"Bloody Indestructible"

The Colour Sergeant delivered some tinned rations, which went under the name of 'Compo' and which we had not seen before. For months our combat ration had been of the 'K' type made up in the USA. These came in wax packets containing small tins (about one and a half inches in diameter) of pork and beans, jam, bacon and egg and similar mixtures. Included in each container were two Camel or Lucky Strike cigarettes and a couple of matches. The wax wrappers would burn like a miniature camp fire, long enough to heat up a mug of water for making tea. But this usually tasted foul and we preferred our own brew boiled in seven-pound jam tins in which we dipped our sodden, stewed tea leaves. The Compo came in large tin containers and was supposed to provide sustenance for one day for fourteen men, or some such arrangement. We liked these victuals because of the tinned fruit and decent biscuits they contained. Bread was an unheard-of thing amongst front line troops in Burma, but we had got used to going without it. Our main requirement was liquids, and our appetite for solid food was easily appeased by whatever we did get. This is not to say we were never hungry: as it happens our main concern at all times was the fact that we felt half-starved. I think our stomachs must have shrunk to compensate for the lack of bulk. Anyway most of us were as thin as rakes: when a man stripped off his shirt one wondered how the skinny frame found the strength enough to hump all the ironmongery necessary to our trade. What wouldn't we have given for a mess tin full of stew and potatoes and fresh greens?

As we sat cleaning our weapons, smoking, chewing on our rations and idly chatting, we gazed back towards the river-crossing zone, where an almost regular ferry service had been established. Despite the events of the past two days and nights, all the activity

down there was reassuring to us and no longer did the small bridgehead seem quite such a terrifying patch of alien territory. How
much longer we could expect it to remain that way, when the enemy
had had time to move up his main forces against us, was a matter
for conjecture.

Peter and I lounged near a trench overlooking the Irrawaddy
shore: we were working out a plan for retrieving our Bren guns and
other equipment which still lay down near the water's edge.

Suddenly we heard the sound of aircraft engines. At first we
thought the approaching planes were Typhoons or Hurricanes but,
as they came nearer, the high-powered roar sounded strangely alien
yet tinny, like accelerating motor-cycle engines; then we spotted the
blood-red circle on the wings and fuselage. They were Jap Zero
fighter-bombers. Everyone grabbed his weapons in an almost light-
hearted fashion and milled around, hoping to watch the fun and
perhaps get in a pot shot or two. It was obvious the target would be
the boats and rafts on the ferry service, not us. One by one the
Zeros peeled off from a tight formation and dived screeching and
vibrating towards the ferries. Anti-aircraft guns on the northern
side of the river crackled madly, filling the sky around the attacking
aircraft with tracer shells and yellow puff-balls of high explosive.
There was a frightening drum-roll of sound as the Zeros' machine-
guns opened up, and we watched the steel hail of bullets hem-stitch
into the river and along the sandy foreshore. Everyone was shooting at the Zeros as they performed an amazing array of aerobatics
above the bridgehead and the river. Seven or eight low-level
attacks, culminating in bombs being dropped harmlessly into the
water, was all they managed to achieve. One could see the
helmeted and goggled heads of the pilots quite clearly. The sound of
their rattle-trap motors clattering in a sort of mechanical rage
seemed to symbolise the enemy's frustration. Here we were
firmly ensconced on the southern shore of the Irrawaddy which
they had sworn to defend to the death.

Quite suddenly it was all over, neither side having done more
than bare its teeth. The Zeros reformed hurriedly and made off
the way they had come. Minutes later a lone Spitfire hurtled
after them at tree-top height and rapidly disappeared from
view.

The incident worked like an enema on a good many of us.

Soon there was a general coming and going through the scrub with entrenching tools at the ready.

Later it occurred to me that the air raid, although bearing its own particular brand of terror, had acted as a catharsis in more ways than one. We had been able to see the enemy clearly and retaliate and we had the sanctity of our trenches and comforting nearness of comrades around us. Somehow it helped to rid our thoughts of the horror of the grenade battle during the night, and morale was once again restored by just the right amount.

After the evening stand-to I took a party out onto the beach and retrieved our belongings and weapons, together with the bodies of the men killed in the ambush.

The business of digging ourselves into our defensive perimeter on the extreme and isolated corner of the bridgehead was now as complete as we could make it. One or two mortar and artillery fire tasks had been laid on to give us close support. Several hundred yards of flat dry river-bed separated us from the remainder of the Battalion. This fact was very much in the forefront of our thoughts, especially when darkness cast its cloak of anxiety and nervous tension upon us once more.

It was almost midnight when the Japanese attacked again. Silently at first they surrounded the Company. Then having boxed us off from the main body, they proceeded to grenade and mortar us relentlessly once more. Despite our own mortar and artillery support the Japs managed to bring up more troops, who by-passed us. Then they opened mass attacks on the main Battalion position behind us. At one point they almost succeeded in breaking through to Battalion HQ.

In the early hours more enemy reinforcements joined them by the simple, if foolhardy, expedient of floating themselves down the Irrawaddy in rubber assault-boats. This lot attempted to break into the rear of the bridgehead: using flame-throwers, they tried to burn the companies out of the long grass.

4·2-inch mortars, from the artillery positions north of the river, gave unceasing support throughout the night. The storm of bombs crashed and whirled about us as we cowered in the sheltering earth. Tiny pieces of metal spanged and sizzled against our steel helmets. Grenades plunged amongst us, their concussion throwing Dick Florence and me this way and that, forward and backward. The earth heaved and shook; Very lights spun up into the sky, poised and floated down; tracers from the Jap machine-guns flared a few feet above our heads, stopped and went on again.

I dug into the side of the trench with my hands, holding myself tense against the awful dithering and shaking of my whole body. My teeth chattered and I felt scalding tears on my cheeks and the salty taste of them on my lips. The appalling crashes and blossoms of flame went on and on. I went down on my knees at the bottom of the trench.

"God, please, stop it! Stop it! No more! no more!"

Near dawn the shooting did stop suddenly.

There was the sound of boots scuffling in the sand. Dick and I wriggled upwards: we could see nothing. Then we heard the sounds of men running in the undergrowth. A white parachute flare spluttered and began to float eerily across the Company. Muffled voices, and then a horrid scream came out of the half dark. Figures blundered about in the scrub. For a long time after that Dick and I stood, rifles held ready, but no one came.

Just before it got fully light, Dick sank to the bottom of the trench and lit a cigarette under his half-blanket. His voice came to me from a long way off:

"I think they've packed up, sir. It'll be full light in a few minutes."

Gradually I relaxed and stretched out my fingers. I flexed my limbs and stretched my legs on either side of Dick, showering him with fine dust and sand.

Closing my eyes for a second, I prayed in an agony of relief. Dick shook himself free of the clawing grass roots in the trench and stood up beside me. We watched the sun rise together. Every incident of the six dark hours of hell we had just endured kept coming back to me. Suddenly I felt cold in my stomach. Turning, I looked at Dick's face streaked with grime and sweat. As though reading my thoughts, he said:

"Christ! we'd better go and see!"

We picked our way carefully through the grenade craters and the dawn mist towards the perimeter trenches. We gazed around . . . and then they began to appear, the other men of the Company – rising out of the ground – like ghosts. Bayonets glinted in the morning sunlight.

A voice behind me said: "You're bloody indestructible."

It was Peter. His face was cracked in a mask-like grin. At first I did not recognise this old man of twenty-six with the waxen skin and red-rimmed sunken eyes.

Dick looked steadily past us into space, his face blank and solemn, his fingers playing idly with the safety-catch of his rifle. Turning his head at last he spoke quietly to Peter.

"That's it, sir, for a bit! You mun get us a bit o' relief after this. *Duw, Duw!*"

From the huddle of shapes, hunched in the black holes amongst the trampled grass, seemed to emanate a sudden overwhelming longing for some concrete consolation – some spark of human understanding to bolster our trembling spirits.

Suddenly the shrill whooping zing of ricocheting bullets cut through the misty morning air.

A handful of Japanese had been too slow in withdrawing. Too late now, they were caught by the dawn light and the rifles in the Battalion perimeter. Crouching behind some upturned country boats near the water's edge at the mouth of the chaung, they were in full view of 'B' Company. At a range of two hundred yards, it would have been easy for us to nail them with our own Brens. But no one even made the attempt. Ironically the tables were turned on the Japanese. Afterwards we all remarked on the coincidence which placed a few of the enemy in practically the identical position where, we ourselves had walked like sheep to the slaughter on that first morning in the bridgehead. On that occasion the Japanese machine-guns had been sited almost exactly where we ourselves now lay.

We watched hypnotised as the skirmish was re-enacted with the enemy on the receiving end. Bombs from a platoon mortar bracketed the country boats. Before the sky-blown sand had settled, one of the Japanese made a break towards the river in a bandy-legged, crouching run. A burst of fire from a Bren brought him to his knees at the water's edge and we watched him scrabbling on all fours for his life. Another Jap ran out: somehow he got the first man across his back and staggered with him towards the spurious cover of the boats. Dick put his hand on my shoulder and leaned forward shouting:

"By damn! Did you see that? Man! Lakri Woods couldn't have done better."

Another salvo of mortar bombs plopped into the damp sand and we could almost feel their scything effect, as the dull reverberating explosions carried to us across the beach. Four or five men from the Battalion climbed out of their trenches on the chaung bank beyond the Japanese. They began to advance slowly, bayoneted rifles at the ready. With less than thirty yards to go, one of the men threw a grenade amongst the motionless group of crumpled khaki-clad Japanese. The section rushed forward yelling, rifle butts swung back, sun flashed on downward lunging bayonets . . . back, down, back, too many times. Like spectators at some gladiatorial combat we watched the *coup de grace* . . .

No doubt, front-line soldiers are prone to over-identification with their adversaries. It is a difficult, almost impossible emotion to define. Certainly as 'B' Company watched this incident, there was an aura of sympathy and understanding. But the men in the section which did the job were functioning on a different emotional wavelength. In such moments the overwhelming instincts of anger and self-preservation either send men sprawling to the ground or sweep them forward to kill with hideous, monstrous voice. It is then that one finds out what is in mankind, lying dormant under the façade of civilisation. Only as a spectator or armchair reader is one tempted to point the thumb upwards and allow the nobly vanquished to live.

There below us in the haze of the rising sun lay the tattered, doll-like figures of the 'Dushman' – the enemy who had come to kill us in the night. Now they were themselves dead men – brave men – and we had watched them die . . .

Rarely did the Japanese leave his dead on the battle-field, especially not during a night attack. On this occasion our defensive fire had been too fierce, too prolonged even for him. The perimeter patrols found the bodies of more than fifty Japanese: they came back to the lines laden with Samurai swords, light machine-guns, and weapons of all kinds, including three of the enemy's medium machine-guns. All of these had been gathered up within a few dozen yards of our front trenches. Amongst the debris of equipment, packs, steel helmets and shattered corpses were scattered thousands of bank-notes. Unfortunately this was merely occupation money, which the Japanese printed themselves for use in the countries which they had overrun. There were cheap tin cigarette-cases amateurishly etched with scenes of battle in China. Simple picture postcards of Mount Fuji-Yama and illustrated diaries and snapshots of young soldiers in tropical settings lay amongst the corpses. Practically every one of the dead Japs had a cheap watch strapped to his wrist, and they all smelt of iodine, cheap scented soap and urine.

The sun had barely begun to warm us when the uncanny silence of the aftermath of battle was rudely shattered. Before the skirmish on the beach I had noticed a young soldier rocking back and forth on his heels, crying to himself quietly on the edge of a trench. Now his voice was pitched high on a note of near hysteria.

"We've 'ad it," he kept shouting. "I ain't stayin' 'ere no longer. Why don't we fuck off 'art of it?"

"Shut your bleedin' mouth!" This from Mason, a burly ex-policeman. "We're staying here . . . an' so are you, yer bastard!"

Sergeant Florence rubbed a hand over his chin. It made a harsh rasping sound.

"Shut up, Mason. Can't you see the kid's bomb-happy?"

The morose lantern-jawed Mason staggered to his feet, using his rifle like a crutch.

"What about me then, Sar'nt? . . . me fukkin' career's ruined."

With this sudden surge of spirit from Mason we discovered that he had a gun-shot wound through his right foot and another through the ankle, both received hours earlier.

We patrolled and pushed out feelers into the surrounding scrub-land and that night the Japanese remained quiet.

FOURTEEN

Alethaung and Tanks

About a mile east of our positions on the bank of the Irrawaddy was the village of Alethaung. We knew that sooner or later it would be our next objective.

In the morning 'A' Company came over the chaung, accompanied by the CO and his defence platoon. Soon afterwards a squadron of light tanks followed. Peter Clark said:

"Thank your lucky stars it's not us this time. I don't fancy being in Terry Hodgson's boots."

Terry gave out his order, not just to an 'O-Group', but to the whole of 'A' Company squatting around him in the dunes. He was probably one of the most consistently successful Company commanders in the Brigade and had won his MC the previous year in one of the terrible battles on the Shenan Ridge. His Company tactics were always good and the men trusted him implicitly as a superb and courageous soldier. Campion, the Company second-in-command, and the only other officer, had been with 'A' Company since the Kabaw valley and their methods were the same.

Terry ended his orders on a note of professional matter-of-factness after the usual 'any questions'?

"Right then: we've come a long way together, but we still have a long way to go. Let's get to it."

With that he waved his hand to Peter and me and led 'A' Company off towards Alethaung. The squadron of tanks went after them, leaving a pall of dust.

An hour or two later we heard the noise of the preliminary barrage and, throughout the hazy afternoon, the distant sounds of bursting bombs and the tearing rattle of machine-guns.

Sergeant Carter, whom I had known in the training battalion at home, was amongst the first of the wounded brought back along the track past 'B' Company's command post. I gave him a cigarette. He was shaking violently in reaction after the bayonet assault.

"Thanks a lot, sir. I could do with a spit 'n' a draw. You know," he went on rapidly, "I feel right pissed. The buggers had me pinned in a foxhole with this one through me leg – I thought I'd never have the strength to crawl, leave alone walk. Then I took a swig at the platoon rum bottle and bloody near sprinted the whole way back."

Soon after that a tank came back with more wounded hanging on like grim death to the bucking steel monster as it roared up the rutted track. The tank stopped near a posse of stretcher-bearers, who stood ready to transfer the wounded men onto jeep ambulances. Campion was amongst the wounded: I helped to lift him down. He was pretty far gone, with machine-gun bullets in the lower abdomen, and he was still unconscious. We were told that he had been hit whilst standing on top of a tank and attempting to direct its fire at an enemy strongpoint. We heard later that he died before he could be got back across the river to an advanced dressing station.

Just after this Peter Gillam came back and told us that 'A' Company were in Alethaung. Peter's command of the Battalion had been confirmed officially that day, although he had been acting as CO since soon after Satpangon. His first command was a pretty depleted one, very low in officers. He told us that he was disbanding 'D' Company and distributing the men amongst the other three companies. Not long afterwards RSM Pope marched those allotted to us across the chaung. Then we moved up in support of Terry and his men in Alethaung. On our way forward some walking wounded from 'A' Company passed us on the track. Battle-drunk and reeling, they were helping each other along and still carrying their personal weapons, though some were without shirts, packs or equipment, and one even without trousers. The CO appeared again and showed us our Company area, after which we lost no time in digging in.

The tanks were a short way ahead beyond the outskirts of the village. They were still under fire from the Japanese. The tank boys were due to come back soon, before it got dark, or they would have been sitting ducks. In any case their fuel and ammunition reserves were back near the ferry crossing.

Sometime before stand-to I was on my way over to Battalion

HQ. I passed some of the 'A' Company men putting the finishing touches to their trenches in the middle of the perimeter, where the CO had placed them in reserve. Earlier in the day they had been timorously expectant: they were laughing now, not with the easy ripple of ordinary men, but with a discordant mad ring which chilled my ears and made me think that the great strain on mind and body must have affected them.

The whole Brigade was now across the river and the bridgehead had been consolidated to a depth of over half a mile, with a base along the river line of nearly two. The periphery of the bridgehead was not held in a continuous line, as one might imagine. The three battalions held the perimeter in blobs centred on villages freshly captured from the Japanese. We held these villages in all-round defence. By night the areas on all sides of the battalions became no-man's-land. For the remaining weeks of the battle almost all the fighting took place during the hours of darkness.

We converted many of the Japanese bunkers in Alethaung to our own use and, as the days went by, connected them with communicating trenches and improved them in other ways to suit our own dispositions. It was as well that we did. Had we but known it, we were about to be thrown *completely* on the defensive.

Darkness came all too soon that first night in our new positions in Alethaung, and with it the Japanese.

Very soon the enemy had built up sufficient strength around the bridgehead to begin counter-attacking in earnest.

At first small squads of storm troops were used to test our strength and determine exactly where our sub-units were located. Contrary to our own tactics on reconnaissance, the Jap sought to gain his information by terrorising us with ferocious small attacks and by uttering piercing screams. Later came the mass charges, with bugles blowing, and the battle cries of "*Tennoheika Banzai*!" "Long live the Emperor!" "Hooray!"

One of the weapons the Japs used most adroitly was a tiny 75-mm field piece, an infantry gun which could be man-handled easily in forward positions and fired over open sights at point-blank range. We nicknamed the shells from these guns 'whizz-bangs' – you would never have time to hear the one that hit you.

Fighting around the whole bridgehead became fiercer, as each enemy reinforcement arrived to be thrown into the attack piece-meal.

The CO was determined that we should dominate no-man's-land and also continue to improve our defensive positions by every possible means. An unusual result of this policy occurred when he sent Robin Gordon's Assault Pioneers out. They were to lay a mine-field and booby-trap a line of trees beyond a gully which the Japanese had begun to use regularly as a forming-up area for their night attacks.

I went with Robin in command of a detail to provide a covering force for the work. Jim Hollier, was even further forward, out to a flank with a small 'recce party' and a high-powered wireless set. His task was to keep an eye out for marauding Japs, who seemed to pop up all over the place when least expected. The job was completed, and Robin and I were chatting and enjoying a smoke when without warning bullets thumped into the bank of earth at the back of the gully. One of our Bren guns opened up at something. Corporal But-terworth appeared with a rather stupified expression on his face and an unlit cigarette stuck to his lower lip: it flicked up and down as he shouted at us excitedly:

"Come on, quick – tanks, Jap tanks!"

Stumbling out of the gully hastily we ran for the nearest vantage point from which we could survey the surrounding countryside. About five hundred yards away, through the early morning heat haze, we saw the menacing shapes fanning out and making towards us, engines snarling softly, heaving and bucking like small ships on a running tide.

Robin counted nine light tanks through his binoculars. He said:

"Jim Hollier should have the Hurri-bombers onto that lot any minute . . . unless the beggers have scuppered him already."

In front of the tanks, rather bunched up, were two lines of Jap infantry advancing steadily with rifles at the trail. Somewhere in the middle was a flag dipping up and down and we could see the red circle plainly. This was the first and only time I ever saw a full-scale attack carried out in daylight by the Japanese.

My rifle sections and Robin's men were by this time lining the gully behind us and we could hear Butterworth shouting fire orders. As it happened, we were somewhere near the middle of one of our defensive fire task areas. We would most probably have pulled back inside the Battalion perimeter then and there. But the tanks were firing steadily with their machine-guns and it would have been extremely foolhardy to get out of the sheltering gully into the open.

We could see the shirt-sleeved Japs dodging about in and out of the scrub now about three or four hundred yards away. An officer or senior WO was ambling along as though on a country walk, a naked sword sloped across his shoulder. From time to time he would wave the sword about from side to side as if directing the operations of the tanks.

My eyes smarted, my throat was dry, and I found myself soaked in sweat. Vaguely I wondered if Robin had noticed how jittery I was. Along the bank to our left a man sagged, crumpled and fell back. One of the Assault Pioneers suddenly climbed out of the gully and started running to the rear. Robin let out a stream of expletives, ran up the bank after him, and raised his rifle as if about to shoot the man down. Next there was a dull slapping sound. Robin let out a terrible oath. Spinning round he fell back clutching his left arm.

Everyone crouched even lower, as bullets cracked above our heads and smacked into the earth around us.

Robin sat up cursing, his hand and arm dripping blood. I turned back and continued firing with the others as targets presented themselves. My rifle bolt stuck fast, fouled with grit. I tore it out somehow, swearing, and licked it clean, spitting out the grit. The metal was hot and scorched my tongue. I glanced once more at Robin. His face in the sunlight was bloodless and dirty; there were streaks of grime on his cheeks where sweat had dried, and a growth of dark beard gave his eyes a strangely animal look. He sat in the sand rocking back and forth, watching us anxiously. The tanks were in the open now, not more than two hundred yards distant. A flight of Hurricanes swept low across the river behind us. In line astern they swooped in shallow dive, barely skimming the line of trees in front of the gully.

A tremendous clamour broke out amongst the scrub and paddy, as the Jap tanks and infantry caught the full fury of the air-crafts' rockets and machine-guns. The enemy could not have been more surprised and dumbfounded than we were ourselves at the speed and suddenness of the attack. Again and again the aircraft saturated the area with their blasting rocket fire. Their screaming dives shocked and deafened us. Hardly had the dust settled before a second flight screamed into the attack. The howl of steel terror descended the scale in a split second: it was as if some giant hand of great power came tearing into the earth. The line of trees ahead of us swayed and groaned; great baulks of timber swayed and crashed to the ground. The air became choked with fine grey dust. Flurries of steel and fragments of sod and stone were tearing into the bushes and across the grass, as if driven by a high wind sucking and hurling the blast. Out ahead petrol fires blazed up in the tanks and ammunition began to explode in them.

Then the air attack stopped all at once. The uproar continued in the paddy, where the fires and exploding ammunition roared and crackled from burning tanks. The bullet-ridden body of a Jap lay collapsed grotesquely across the can-opened turret of one of them. The planes roared overhead again, the lettering on the underside of their fuselages clearly visible. We stood up, minds working, to seek a way of escape in case they had mistaken us for the enemy.

An engine screamed: it was coming straight at us in the gully. Men swore and cried out, flinging themselves sideways and even climbing into the open. Then the plane soared, banked and turned away, waggling its wings.

The men who had run for it jumped back down amongst us swearing with relief. Robin was standing now, one arm round the shoulder of his batman, the other arm like a broken wing hanging loosely by his side. A blood-lipped gash lay open wide from elbow to wrist. I caught his glazed, deep-set eyes.

"Close enough for you, cobber?" he asked quietly.

"Too fukkin' close for me," said his batman.

"It's bleedin' well not done yet," shouted Butterworth.

A plane had turned and was diving again. Down it came, on exactly the same path, howling out of the morning sun.

"This is our bleedin' lot," I heard Butterworth groan. He was on his knees at the bottom of the gully, as if in prayer.

Our hearts sank. Again we grovelled. As we closed our eyes and tensed ourselves at the approaching roar, the plane pulled up, banked and soared away. We looked up: it showed its belly to us like some monstrous attacking fish.

"Get us out of here, Coop, for Christ's sake! What the hell are we waiting for?" groaned Robin. For the first time since he was hit he was feeling the pain of the wound.

After that we just got up and shambled back to Alethaung, without even a backward glance at the carnage in the blackened paddyfields.

FIFTEEN

Boy Scouts and White Tigers

Another unit in the Brigade had got a prisoner and it looked as if the Japanese facing us were the 33rd (Sendai) Division. When this particular division had failed to break through into Imphal the previous year it had lost heavily: but its constant suicidal attacks had been so remarkable in their boldness, even for the Japanese, that it had been no surprise when we discovered that it was regarded as a 'crack' division. There can be few examples in history of a force as reduced, battered and exhausted as the Sendai division continuing to deliver such furious assaults; and this, not in order to fight its way out of an untenable position to save its skin, but in order to achieve the original objectives set for it. It was obvious that here, behind the Irrawaddy river line, the Sendai Division was as determined and as fanatical as ever and, more than likely, reinforced with troops of the same calibre.

One morning, after a typical suicidal charge, and despite the numbers of dead the Japanese had undoubtedly managed to retrieve, bulldozers were used to bury more than seven hundred Japanese corpses in mass graves along the Brigade front.

Major General Tanaka, the Sendai Divisional Commander, is reputed to have stated later that during this period two of his battalions delivered attacks against the bridgehead perimeter with a strength of 1200 men each, only to lose 953.

One of his storm regiments was the redoubtable 214 Infantry, the Byaka Tai – or White Tiger Band, as they called themselves – and they were probably the most ferociously barbarous bunch of soldiers ever to wear a uniform in the history of modern warfare.

I am not ashamed to say that they regularly scared the living daylights out of me, at any rate.

This phase of the bridgehead battle was almost purely an infantry affair – often hand to hand, man against man, and no quarter.

One exception to this state of affairs will serve to demonstrate how a resourceful commander was able to turn the enemy's hidebound and repetitive tactics to his own advantage. The 4th/10th Gurkhas' Commanding Officer was Lieutenant Colonel Vickers. He was known affectionately throughout the 100th Indian Infantry Brigade as the Chief Boy Scout. This nickname probably arose from the fact that Colonel Vickers, along with all his officers and men, disdained the use of steel helmets. Even under shell-fire you could see the soldiers of the 4th/10th still wearing their peculiarly flat-brimmed, well blocked and carefully crimped bush-hats at a suitably rakish angle.

One of the Chief Boy Scout's platoons held a position in a small copse which was constantly attacked by large parties of enemy. Each time the Japs came in the Chief Boy Scout withdrew the platoon back into the main perimeter of his battalion. The moment the enemy were installed in the copse he called down a pre-arranged defensive artillery barrage of such intensity that the Japs were practically decimated. The barrage would lift, and in would go the Chief Boy Scout at the head of his Gurkhas to finish off any who remained alive. Then a platoon would be left in the copse once more until the next attack, when it would be withdrawn again and the whole proceedings repeated.

Given specific orders, the Japanese rarely, if ever, seemed capable of adapting their tactics to suit the circumstances. The Chief Boy Scout knew this very well and made excellent use of the knowledge. Night after night we used to listen in our trenches on the left flank of the Gurkhas' sector of the bridgehead while the macabre concert was re-enacted, with monotonous regularity. Sometimes the Japanese and the Chief Boy Scout would lay on an afternoon matinee as well. One morning in the copse – an area less than 50 yards square – the Gurkhas counted more than five hundred enemy dead.

Now that Robin had been evacuated, John Margarson and myself and Jim Hollier, who had somehow survived the aircraft-tank battle with his standing patrol, were the only remaining subalterns left in command of rifle platoons. In fact we were Company Seconds-in-Command and general dogs' bodies. Not surprisingly we had begun to feel that we were getting far more than our fair share of the war.

While the Japanese counter-attacks were at their height, I personally spent no less than nine consecutive nights, or parts of those
nights, in no-mans-land with patrols, ambushes, and raiding
parties, either of my own men or volunteers from the other companies. I had begun to dread the approach of evening stand-to and
the waiting for the inevitable summons to Company or Battalion
HQ for orders which would send me out again.

By day in the insect-humming tropical sunshine, we dug,
patrolled, improved the defences and tried to sleep under the constant harassing barrages of our own gunfire and the answering
ones of the enemy.

Once we swam, by relays of sections, in the Irrawaddy, with
shells hurtling and shuttling low above the torn trees of Alethaung.
Anti-aircraft sentries nearby scanned the cloudless sky with binoculars.

With the approach of evening the copper-smith bird would begin
its endlessly monotonous knock-knock-knocking somewhere in the
trees; the tuck-too lizard joined in remorselessly, crying its derisive
call to the flaming sunset. A lull would descend over the scene – a
short breathless pause before the terror of the night hours.

A field telephone in its slot in the side of the trench would buzz
demandingly. Dick would pull out the handset and hiss into the
mouthpiece:

"Six platoon, Florence. . . . Yes sir, I'll tell him."

The world seemed to hold its breath. My pores opened
and cold sweat oozed out of me; my hands trembled.

"Christ, not again!"

Knock, knock, knock from the trees nearby; then the
lizard insistently, insanely in time with my own soundless
expletives; Tuck-too! Tuck-too!

"Fuck you too, you mad bastard! Not again! Oh
Christ Jesus, not again!"

Smithie, back with the platoon now for several days,
would look up from his eternal rifle-cleaning.

"Don't let the sods grind you in, boss. Tell the bastards yer goin' sick."

Later, when I returned to my platoon for my things,
he would fuss around me as though I were a helpless
bairn and administer to my needs like an anxious mother

sending her child off to some unspeakably nasty school.

Mesmerised, confused with emotional exhaustion, I would find myself once more outside the ring of steel and flesh which was the Battalion . . . an animal, alert, terrified and crazily vicious.

One night Johnny McQuade, sometime International Brigade soldier in the Spanish Civil War, and now a sergeant in 'C' Company, accompanies me to the bunker which has been dug well out in the scrub, near where the Japanese are wont to form up for their night attacks.

Inside the bunker is a field telephone connected to Battalion HQ. When the Japs come we have to call for artillery fire and mortars. With any luck even a direct hit on ourselves will do little damage – well, anyway, that's what the pioneer sergeant has assured us. There's barely room inside to crouch low enough to see through the observation slits . . . no way out if the Japs catch us inside.

Now and then white parachute flares flood the landscape with an eerie light. The breathless stillness is broken only intermittently by the noise of small-arms fire from the direction of the Gurkha positions on our right.

The night air is sweet with the smell of wood fires. We'd like to talk and smoke and walk around to relieve our cramped limbs: but we daren't relax our vigilance. A few hundred tired men, half of them trying to sleep, are relying on our eyes, our ears, our nerves to warn them.

After what seems an eternity of waiting, Johnny says quietly:

"They're coming up out of the chaung."

He cranks the handle of the field telephone. I hear the sleepy voice at the other end of the line.

"Seagull on set."

My throbbing temples seem ready to burst. Johnny hisses down the mouthpiece:

"Wake up, you bastards. Dog fox one! *Jaldi!*"

I am peering wildly through the observation slit: nothing moves. Then I notice dark shadows, which do. Out of the cool, scented blackness, with whispering shrieks like the wailing of a dozen banshees, the defensive barrage comes down about us. The shelling with its monotonous beat drugs us as we sit five feet down in the quivering earth, staring – at nothing. The Sten gun standing upright between my knees shakes with each concussion. Fountains of flame blaze splitting light, shafting through the observation apertures of the bunker with each explosion.

Outside there is screaming and the high-pitched jabbering of Japanese voices.

A rising and falling circle of red light shows me that Johnny's smoking. I'm too afraid to light a cigarette myself in case, by moving, I break the spell of security created by the feel of the crowding earth against my hands.

All at once I know I am counting the shell bursts.

"Thirty-three, thirty-four . . ."

Dull flat explosions amid the harsher crack of the shell bursts warn us that the mortars have joined in the 'stonk'. They are comparatively harmless to us unless one drops down the entrance hole. But the noise is indescribable. I shout to save my eardrums from bursting. I feel Johnny's hands on my shoulders, and his voice comes from miles away:

"Are you okay?"

"Yeh! Except for a heart attack and a nervous breakdown."

We sit tensely waiting for the shell which will drop on us and cave in the top of the shelter and bury us. Red and orange flashes slash the darkness inside our six-by-two-foot grave. My bladder, distended by the water I've drunk and by fear, gives out: I unbutton and squirm onto my side. I settle back again, sitting in piss with my hands gritty and wet. A mad desire comes over me to push one of my hands through the slit and invite a shell splinter, so that they'll evacuate me. Which hand? Left, you bloody fool!

McQuade slumps forward, his teeth chattering. His lips twitch against the back of my hand and I sense the rising hysteria. I seize him by the shirt and slap his face hard. He jerks back in the pitch blackness.

"You bastard!" he screams. "You dirty, rotten, bloody bastard!"

The barrage lifts momentarily, but then starts up again. Johnny lights another cigarette and passes it to me.

"Here, Ken; have a drag."

Suddenly the deafening noise stops. We wait for an age. When I stop shivering, I examine the luminous dial of my watch. It is 0345 hours.

Later we try the telephone. It's useless – the wires have gone long ago.

The Japs don't come again. Before first light we crawl laboriously out of the bunker. The thought occurs to me that there may be Japs around, moving their dead; but I can hear nothing. I am bloody near completely deaf anyway, and too shell-happy to care much. We walk carefully, eyes popping like organ stops. The acrid smell of burnt explosives makes me want to retch, and we fall repeatedly into shell craters.

On the line nobody challenges our approach. We crawl closer, whispering the password. In the end we just stand up and walk in.

A sentry in a two-man weapon pit is slumped across the parapet with his hands resting on a Bren gun. Using his steel-helmeted head as a stepping stone, I stride across the trench. The sentry rears under me like a panicked steer and lets out a scream to wake the dead. His head goes back and I see the whites of his eyes in the half light. I grab the sod by the hair and slap him backhanded across the mouth.

"You, bloody, murderous bastard! I'll have you shot," I croak at him.

McQuade pulls me off the fellow, and the section corporal appears and puts his bayonet half way up my right nostril.

"Steady on, sir; steady," says McQuade. "Come on, let's get in. Leave this to the corporal." He grabs me firmly by the arm. "That sentry was asleep," he says to the NCO. "I'll come back and do the git when I've had some tea."

We shave and drink tea together in my dug-out, Smithie running round like a mother hen. We don't talk much. I feel vague and dazed like after a nightmare.

"How was it, Sarge?" Smithie asks McQuade, and Johnny answers:

"Believe me, Smudger, it was never like that in Spain . . ."

SIXTEEN

Ambush

Somehow with the sunlight the night's events receded, but I was as jumpy as a cat until the runner came before evening stand-to.

"The Major wants you at Company HQ, sir."

Peter's tone was definitely apologetic when I got there.

"This is an ambush party, Coop. Catch old Jappo in his forming-up area in the chaung; twenty picked men, all volunteers; and you've got Sergeant Winters going with you – good man, professional boxer in civvy. Push off an hour after stand-down."

I knew the chaung well; it was half a mile away. It might just as well have been on the moon, so awesome had no-man's-land become in my thoughts.

I rejoined my platoon. The men in my headquarters were touchingly sympathetic. Jock Lawson had led a recce patrol earlier in the day and been ambushed, losing one of the men with him. He was still very shaken and reacting violently from the experience.

He and I, Bull, Dick, Smithie, Ernie and Bill Hughes and a few of the old bunch had learnt how to stay alive. But we knew deep down that it was just luck. If you stayed alive as long as we had, you were lucky. It was not a matter of not taking chances. We felt certain each time we went out we were going to catch the one with our name stamped on it. When we came back, we marvelled at our own luck, and if things let up a bit we convinced ourselves we were indestructible; that they had not made the one for us yet. We kept on going back because we were more scared of our pals thinking we were no bloody good than we were of the chances of stopping one.

I had long since become prey to superstition and carried lucky charms in my pocket. I used to adopt certain ways of putting on clothes and equipment, for fear that if I stopped doing things like that, the magic sequence of survival would evaporate.

Jock asked:

"Do you ever feel like disobeying orders?"

"Yeh, – when the crazy bastards give the wrong orders."

It was forced, but it broke the tension and Jock knew what I meant.

The relationship between the men in rifle platoons and those further back, even company quartermaster sergeants, was a delicate one. LOB meant 'Left out of battle'. We were not really bitter, just snobbish. It was only in the waiting time we gave the matter much thought; you need leisure for real thinking. Leisure was something the little men at the sharp end never had.

I went off to get myself ready. The waiting time was always the worst: that was when the neurosis built up. I tried not to think, but the usual premonitions came crowding in. The final half hour you lived on nerves only. Several times my thoughts wandered to the bottle of 'hooch' in my pack, which Peter had given to me the day before in a moment of over-indulgence. There was nothing to do. We smoked, Smithie and I, under the screen of our blankets. You could always pick out the front-line soldier by the nicotine stains on the palm of his hand from shielding the red glare of his fag-end from Japs and the prying eyes of field officers.

"Smudge,"

"Yeh, boss?"

"Empty my water bottle and shove that whisky into it; save a swig for yourself." Smithie hesitated.

"Now look, kid . . ."

"Cut out the bloody mammie lark, Smithie, and get me that plonk."

He sighed heavily, resignedly.

"OK, boss man . . . it's your funeral."

The purpled light faded quickly and somewhere over the Gurkha lines a machine-gun rattled.

Our feet moved automatically. The patrol filed silently behind Winters and me through the shell craters and in and out of the stifling closeness of the crowding scrub.

We pointed out a rendezvous to the men near some country boats thirty yards from the chaung.

A track led into the chaung and out the other side towards Kalewa, a Jap stronghold half a mile to the south. We laid the ambush near a bend in the track where the scrub offered some cover.

Then Winters and I went and sat under a stunted, heavily foliaged umbrella tree with our heads against the trunk. We were about ten paces behind the men in the centre of the ambush position.

Sometime later I remembered the whisky in my water bottle. "Just one swig", I told myself, and passed the bottle to Winters. An hour later, on the hour, we took another swig each.

"That's it," I thought. "Every hour on the hour won't do any harm and it's dead quiet so far."

By three in the morning I was ready to fight General Tanaka and his 33rd Division single-handed! I wondered why no Japs had appeared all night. Soon afterwards we heard the Jat Regiment's guns: the Vickers were dug in on our perimeter. They had cut loose at something with several long bursts.

Very lights began to spin up into the blue-black sky. From well over on our right a lazy burst of tracer bullets sailed up, up and over our heads. From the direction of the Battalion perimeter came the dull thud-thud of exploding hand grenades.

Slowly I crept along the ambush line from one position to the next. Ten pairs of pale faces peered up from the dusty earth.

"All right?"

"All right, sir."

"*Thik hai.* Keep your eyes skinned."

Wondering what was happening in Alethaung, I crept back along the ambush line. Most likely a jitter party, I concluded. Back under the umbrella tree, Winters was trying to be sick without making a noise.

A big white cheese of a moon was flitting in and out of towering banks of cloud and alternately lighting and blacking out the scene around us like someone operating an electric light switch in a heavily curtained room.

Then the Japs came along the track from the wrong direction!

They were chattering quite loudly and moving fast when I became aware of their presence. I froze in my tracks. One of them saw me and let out a startled yell. He bounded off rapidly straight across the track in front of the men in the ambush.

The rest of the Japs went after him like greased lightning in their rubber-soled, split-toed patrol socks. The whole thing happened so quickly and unexpectedly that no one on either side fired a single shot. I don't believe that more than two of our men even saw the Japs and there must have been at least two dozen of them.

But we all knew what would happen next if we didn't move double quick. Winters came out of that umbrella tree like a grey-hound out of a trap. He let out a piercing whistle, with two fingers in his mouth. Seconds later the men belted back and Winters led them on to the RV. I counted them as they came through.

"Quick! Move, move, move your bloody feet! He'll mortar this track any minute."

A split second later there was an appalling crash and blossom of flame not twenty yards from me. I tucked my head into the ground. Another bomb landed – nearer this time – and I felt the hot blast hit my back and shoulders. The last two men came out of their position like the proverbial shit off a shovel. They passed me cursing, arms going like pistons. Then I was up on my feet. Almost before Winters had rallied the patrol beyond the country boats, I had caught them up giggling drunkenly.

Two hundreds yards away, between us and the Battalion, a 3-inch mortar bomb burst. Winters groaned.

"What the fukkin' 'ell are they playing at now? They know we're still out here."

"Spread out, for Christ's sake!" I shouted. "Spread out and lie doggo."

The Jap mortar bombs were dropping all over the place by this time. Seconds afterwards the Battalion 3-inch mortars settled down into a steady beat of defensive fire behind us.

The slap and crash of the Jap knee-mortars stopped suddenly. Figures began flitting between the trees and bushes near where our ambush had been.

Many things happened at once after that. One of my Bren guns cut loose, and I knew we were in for a fire-fight at the very least.

"Why couldn't the silly sod have kept quiet?"

I fired a white Very light. It poised and fell. The running shapes of the Japanese could be seen weaving and dodging in the scrub.

A bright glow of tracer filled the sky. Bullets spanged amid the trees and cracked into the country boats. Most of us had fortunately given these a wide berth. But the Japs obviously thought that was where we were and concentrated most of their fire in that direction.

There was a movement in the scrub not ten yards distant and then a lot of shouting. Suddenly I saw Winters standing up with another man, an old soldier whose name I forget. They began hurling grenades into the undergrowth from where the shouting had come. Green, blue and red tracers flared out from the Jap gun, and then Winters screamed:

"Charge, charge! Come on, into the bastards! Chaaaaarge!"

Figures milling about in the moonlight. Me lurching to my feet. Winters drunkenly balling:

"Show 'em yer cap badge, Border."

Men on either side of me shouting and running and firing Sten guns from the hip.

A gigantic Japanese appeared directly in my path. I swear the sod looked seven feet tall, with an arse like a carthorse. He held his arms outstretched like a Suamo wrestler. I ran at him snarling like a mad-dog, going for his gut with the muzzle of my rifle. Before I could squeeze the trigger, I felt a blinding crack on the side of my face and the taste of blood in my mouth.

I must have turned completely over in the air before landing on my knees, grovelling and spitting blood and teeth. My face was buried in the dust. Someone had stood on my head and trampled me flat. There was a horrid sound midway between a cough and a choke and a heavy body fell across my legs, quivered, threshed and then lay still.

The firing had stopped and there were only muffled voices around me. Thankfully I recognised they were speaking English.

I wriggled free of the dead weight which held me pinned to the earth. Then I saw him – a stinking brown animal-man in tattered khaki rags. His life blood spurted out of his neck in great gushes onto my hands and legs. Somehow I gained my feet and spewed all over the dying Japanese.

The old soldier pulled me to the ground beside him and put a fatherly hand round my shoulder.

"Keep yer 'ead down, son. They've not gone yet," he said in a calm matter-of-fact voice.

We lay and waited and I wondered if he could feel my body shaking.

It was still and quiet. A faint breeze rustled in the trees. When I decided to move, the patrol was loath to approach the perimeter trenches. Somebody whispered to Winters:

"I'll bet them trigger-happy Indian machine-gunners give us the chop any minute."

In the end Winters and I and the old soldier crawled closer and began to whistle the National Anthem. There was no reply: so we tried again with the regimental march, "John Peel". We were so off key it could have been "Alexander's Rag Time Band". A voice shouted the password:

"Fuck-'em-all-bar-two."

Winters and the old soldier walked across to the sentry and I heard them chanting the countersign:

"That's me and you."

I brought up the others, who were carrying two men across their rifles, one dead and the other too badly hurt to walk.

The trenches in my platoon's front-line position were a haven of comfort and security. The men told me later that I slept through stand-to and the first hour after dawn with my eyes wide open. Movement around my platoon HQ brought me half awake. Then I heard Bullard conversing with Smithie.

"Cut his boots off, Smudger, and I'll give you a hand to bury the poor bleeder."

SEVENTEEN

Admonished

Through the stupor of my confused senses I could hear the field telephone ringing and then Florence speaking to someone on the other end of the line.

"Yes, its me, sir. Sergeant Florence . . . yea, he's here at the command post. But he's dead beat . . . what's that? Jesus he's going to do his nut . . . All right, sir, I'll tell him."

By the time this one-sided conversation terminated I was fully awake, on my feet and filled with apprehension at what it might presage.

"CO's on the bloody warpath, sir . . . that was the Company Commander. Says the Old Man wants to know why your patrol came back early. He's had no report, except from Charlie Company, who let you back in at 0400 after some bloody awful shemozzle had been going on."

"What the hell are you talking about?" I almost screamed at Dick. "What the blazes does he mean, *early*?"

Rage boiled up inside me and in a blind fury I stumbled, running towards the Battalion command post, cursing incoherently.

Wrenching aside a tattered blanket hanging over the entrance of the deep dug-out, I hurled myself down the earth ramp in a shower of dust and small stones. When my eyes became accustomed to the smoke-filled gloom inside, I found myself confronting Colonel Gillam. Terry Hodgson, his newly appointed Second-in-Command, was there too, together with David Kitchen, the Adjutant, and two men from the signal section. They all seemed more than somewhat surprised at my unceremonious entrance. Straight away I went into the attack, directing my remarks generally, but trying to look the CO fully in the eyes.

"Right, you bastards! What's this about me coming in early? I go out on ambush without benefit of proper orders, no bloody preparation, perimeter not informed; we get stonked by our own mortars and practically bloody murdered . . . and you want to know why I came back in early; that's the ninth consecutive bloody night I've gone without sleep out there, while you bastards" – at this point I swept my arm round theatrically, embracing Colonels, Adjutants, Regimental Sergeant Majors, the gilded staff and anyone else who could recline in a dug-out all night and expect to wake up in one piece next morning – "while you bastards sit on your fat arses and stick pins into bloody maps."

David was beginning to make noises like an Adjutant. Without pausing for breath I yelled at him:

"And you can get stuffed for a start!"

A broad grin began to crease Terry's face and for the first time I realised what a pathetic fool I must have appeared. I was practically blubbering with frustration. My hair was matted and filthy and there was dried blood itching and cracking on my face and the side of my head. Suddenly my legs wouldn't support me and I could feel my knees twitching uncontrollably. I felt myself subside, still mumbling obscenities, to the floor of the command post. I heard the CO telling the signallers:

"Bugger off out of it, you two, and take those damn silly grins off your faces."

I looked up shamefaced, aware of the CO offering me a cigarette and a stained mug of something.

"Here, sit up. Take a drink of this."

It was tea well laced with rum.

For long minutes he said nothing further, just sat quietly looking at me, concern in his eyes and warming his hands on his own steaming mug. I managed to get my eyes high enough to examine the black rims of his finger nails. When at last he spoke, I was startled and almost spilled the remains of my drink. The CO's tone was unusually quiet, though firm.

"You think I don't know how you're feeling. Let me assure you that I do, only too well. You're all shagged, you want to lie down and you think you can't go on any more . . . you think you hate me more than you hate the Japs! But you will go on, we all will – you, me, everyone of us, until this thing's finished. When you feel more yourself, go back to the Company and get some sleep."

"I'm OK." I said. "Don't know what came over me – thanks; I'm
. . . I'm sorry."

Climbing awkwardly to my feet I made for the dug-out door and
began slowly up the ramp.

"Ken!"

I half turned.

"Sir?"

"You're doing fine and so are those lads of yours. You can tell
them that I appreciate it, believe me. Later on I'll come over and
have a word with them."

I stammered something suitably apologetic.

"Go on, get out," he said. "Oh, and by the way . . . next time you
call me a bastard – smile."

EIGHTEEN

Sindat and More Tanks

Two thousand yards east of Alethaung and also on the river bank stood Sindat, dominating a great bend of the Irrawaddy and the country which lay south, east and west for several miles. From where we were could be seen the immense gold and white pagodas of the township thrusting upwards from the green mantle of trees about their feet. In the strong sunlight the pagoda umbrellas shimmered against the sky – ethereal, mysterious and infinitely menacing. As more men and material were ferried into the bridgehead our thoughts began to focus constantly on Sindat and the Japanese stronghold it contained. We had long since convinced ourselves that it would be one more job for the Battalion.

In the daylight hours, between sporadic shelling, patrolling and the never-ending fatigues, we stood in the trenches about Alethaung and gazed mesmerised across the expanse of no-man's-land towards the compelling prospect of Sindat. Paddy and scrub, brooding and silent under a mirage-provoking haze of heat, spurted now and then with mushrooming clouds of earth and yellow smoke, where exploding shells and mortar bombs disturbed the slumbering tranquillity of the scene. By night the dry, square paddyfields became a chequerboard of deadly gaming pawns, as the enemy and ourselves roamed relentlessly amongst the bunds and chaungs hunting and killing.

At all hours the ceaseless chatter of machine-guns rose and fell around and about the periphery of the bridgehead.

One morning we heard the unaccustomed roar of giant engines and the rumbling and clanking of steel tracks approaching from the west. When a squadron of General Lee tanks harboured nearby, the question which had been uppermost in our minds was answered. All we needed to know then was which company would make the initial assault and how soon.

Peter Clark sounded really apologetic when he sent for me to explain the situation.

"The CO wants that derelict village between here and Sindat searched and cleared as a start-line for the attack on Sindat. They're giving us tanks. Send your best NCO with a section to look the place over before stand-to this evening."

I sent Bill Hughes and his stalwarts. They returned mightily relieved and reported the place deserted.

My orders then were to occupy immediately and remain until relieved. All night and the next day the platoon lay in the derelict village there on the edge of the blistering plain. There was a decomposing cow sharing the position under a basha which I had allotted to Corporal Hughes's section. The air around them was thick with flies. Around mid-afternoon a large patrol of enemy came out of Sindat. At first we thought they might skirt our position: when they did not, we bombed them with 2-inch mortars until they moved off towards their gun positions to the south. After that we prayed that we should be relieved before nightfall. I didn't give much for our chances if the Japs sent a large party over in the dark.

'C' Company turned up eventually and Arthur Whittam, the company commander, asked for our assistance to dig in the sections of 3-inch mortars and medium machine-guns that were with him.

Johnny Margarson was with 'C' Company. Arthur decided to hold the end of the village nearest Alethaung and asked for artillery defensive fire tasks on the other end which faced the Japs.

We stayed on digging until it was almost dark before moving back to the Battalion position.

Back in Alethaung I sipped my tea in the platoon HQ dug-out with Smithie. We had stood down in the last minutes of the day. Then faintly, from the east where we had left 'C' Company, came the sounds of machine-gunning and the dull reverberating thud of hand grenades exploding . . .

In the morning we went over to the tank laager to familiarise ourselves with the technicalities of communication between tank crew and infantry. We were shown the telephones kept in containers under the armour plating at the back of each tank.

No one thought much of the procedure. To approach a tank under fire would invite a scragging from every enemy weapon in the vicinity.

One of the more popular methods we finally agreed on was that of indicating targets for the tank gunners by firing tracer bullets. But the crews were pretty blind behind their steel walls: in the event we expected to be forced on occasion to use the tank telephones anyway. We could imagine ourselves shouting:

"Look here, old man, turn a bit to the left, so that you can see our tracers indicating the target for you."

By mid-day the orders were out for the attack on Sindat. We learnt that 'B' Company had the doubtful honour of leading the assault with 'C' Company in support. As they were already in the derelict village, which had been designated as the forming-up area, we were to move up and through them there. The General Lee tanks were also in support, although not going ahead of us as we had fondly hoped.

Now that we knew, after days of wondering, which company would get the job, it seemed easier to face up to it. I, for one, felt better, perhaps because of the definiteness of it, the certainty that there was no backing down, no escaping. Sindat had by then assumed a sinister prospect out of all proportion in our minds: thoughts of the assault had been nagging at us for a long time. Now the moment had arrived, the feeling that we could at last get on with it came almost as a relief from a nightmare.

After the 'order group' of officers and NCOs was concluded, I called all the men of the platoon together, leaving only sentries on the line. Drawing a map in the dust with the point of my bayonet, I outlined the plan of attack in detail. I went over it again and again until I was confident that each man knew exactly what we were going to do. The tank support was the most reassuring element of information I had had for the men in a long time, but I could see the faraway thoughtfulness in their eyes. I tried to sound as confident and optimistic as possible: but most of the men were veterans – they knew the score all right. When I finished they still looked depressed and in no mood to be jollied along.

Afterwards, near my platoon command post, I came across Sergeant Florence with Jock Lawson, Ernie Morrisroe and Smithie.

They were quietly cleaning their weapons with slow, deliberate movements. They were not talking and they seemed to turn away from me, seeking privacy where there was none. I wondered what thoughts would sustain them through the next hours.

I squatted down with them, almost afraid to speak.

"Those tank boys look pretty hot stuff," I managed at last.

Dick looked up and his eyes flashed with anger.

"We could have managed without being the bloody assault company for a bit longer, couldn't we?"

He paused, looked away and then went on:

"The bastards seem to think that this war out here is just a sodding side-show – they should try cracking a position like Sindat with a couple of half-strength companies – tanks or no bleeding tanks."

"Where's the reinforcements?" asked Ernie. "The Indians and Gurkhas always seem to be up to strength."

"Ay," said Jock quietly; "it's agin the law o' averages. Some o' us ha' used up about eight o' our nine lives a' ready."

Dick turned away, managing a smile. He reached behind him for his rifle and began to clean it again, a thin forlorn figure.

I felt something strong and tender for these fine, kind, brave men who were my friends and who had given me their strength and trust.

Alf Bullard came up, lugging his 2-inch mortar, and joined us.

"I don't care what the personal weapon of a mortar man is 'supposed' to be, Guv; this time I ain't goin' in without a rifle, as well as me bleedin' pea-shooter 'ere."

It was poor old Bull's constant moan that he was wasted as a mortar man: he never missed a chance to remind me that with only a revolver for personal protection he was much more vulnerable than the rest of us; and if there was to be in-fighting I was wasting a man by not arming him properly.

There was a strange kind of excitement as we moved up to the start-line. We came to the derelict village 'C' Company had successfully held against repeated attacks during the night from small but insistent parties of enemy.

The tanks rumbled along behind us, well spread out and sending up a cloud of dust, which alerted the Jap artillery. Soon shells began to land amongst them.

Even those of us who were afraid seemed to find strength enough

to put on a show of bravery. We tried to laugh and joke to hide our
fears. We found courage in the rumbling of our own guns and the
mushrooming explosions as our 25-pounder shells dropped into
Sindat. They wallowed down from the top of their trajectories to
explode amongst the trees shrouding the Japanese positions.

As we passed through 'C' Company, waiting in their trenches, I
saw John Margarson and he walked alongside me for a little way.

"Well," I said, "How do you feel, now that you've pulled the
cushy number in support?"

"All right, I suppose," he grinned; "a little concerned, nevertheless," he went on gravely, "that these paths of glory have a habit of
leading to an old army blanket and a shallow grave."

I laughed and eased my pack and equipment on my shoulders.

"I'm trying not to think of it," I said.

John gave me the old lop-sided grin I had come to expect of him.
He stopped and waved me a casual salute.

"Good luck, Coop."

A small-calibre shell crashed fifty yards away. As I trudged on
with the platoon I heard Johnny shout after me.

"If you stop one of those buggers, you'll be in heaven before the
devil knows you're dead."

Two hundred yards from the start-line the CO halted us, so that
the tanks could negotiate a deep chaung which crossed our front.

All round me men were resting against the paddy bunds, cigarettes hanging from dry lips: many of them began reading crumpled
letters from home. Bull lay some yards away, extracting sloppy
bully beef out of a tin with his jack-knife and dropping bits of meat
into Jock Lawson's out-stretched hand.

"Might as well be generous for once, yer Scotch git. Don't want
you telling Saint Peter yer old mate Bull was a tight bastard, do I?"

The smell of burning oil and exhaust fumes from the tanks was
strong in the air. Behind us, on the other side of the chaung, I could
see the CO standing beside the tank squadron-commander's car-
rier.

"Hope the Old Man's not cadging a lift," said Smithie. "Someone ought to tell him those things are dangerous."

We watched as the first troop of tanks eased down into the
marshy chaung and wondered vaguely if there was a chance they
might get stuck at the bottom.

The bombardment thudded and grumbled and the Jap-held village ahead was eclipsed in coloured smoke and rising dust clouds. Here and there a few fires made pinpricks of light against the olive green curtain of trees. A 3-inch mortar bomb from positions behind the derelict village fell short in the oven-hot air. The blast blew my helmet off and I cursed Mike Morley back on the mortar line, as I held my hands to my singing ears. A few Jap shells came over, aimed no doubt at the tanks, but near enough to us to make us duck and flinch. We moved restlessly as showers of earth and stones were flung up across the paddyfields. The tank squadron was down now, out of sight in the bottom of the chaung. We could hear the engines roaring as flames and blue smoke belched from their exhausts into the air.

We waited expectantly. One tank roared into sight, balanced precariously on the bank of the chaung and slammed forward onto its tracks. It was the leading troop-commander who came over next, head and shoulders exposed above his turret, earphones firmly clamped over the black beret on his head. I stood up and went to his tank a few yards away from the platoon. Looking down into the chaung I was horrified, though hardly surprised, to see the remaining ten tanks of the squadron churning deeper and deeper into the mire. They were stuck fast, hopelessly bogged down, flat on their bellies. The frustrated commanders gesticulated and cursed above the roar of the accelerating engines.

"Biggest balls-up since the Somme," I shouted down at them.

The explosive hissing chatter of machine-guns and the flurry of shelling in front swelled into a tremendous racket as the bombardment reached its climax.

I heard Peter Clark give the order to fix bayonets, and then the hiss and rattle of the scabbards as the blades came away, and the snick as they were locked in place on the rifle muzzles.

Somewhere in the rear a bugle sounded, the clarion notes clear and sweet and urgent in the hot afternoon.

"Advance . . . !"

We began to get up. Dick dropped a box of 2-inch mortar bombs and savagely kicked at it before stooping to pick it up. His helmet lop-sided as he bent forward, and I heard his bitter comment to Smith.

"I knew it, I knew it. Nobody recce'd the route for the tanks. Of all the stupid, jumped-up, shagging balls-ups . . . Oh Jesus, what's the good?"

His lips moved, but no words came. He trudged towards me, shoulders hunched, eyes glazed, unseeing, uncaring. Every man about me seemed isolated in his own loneliness.

Bullets began to crack and hiss about us like a swarm of hornets. Shell-bursts spewed rubble between groups of crouching men. We covered the ravaged dust of no-man's-land in a state of mental suspension, the two tanks amongst us bobbing up and down over the paddy bunds like cavalry at the trot.

I caught sight of Peter away to the left between the other two platoons.

"Out!" he was shouting. "Get out to the right. Take that flaming bunker in the pagodas."

We scrambled on, reforming as we went, and rushed a Jap position which was isolated a hundred yards to the right of the village among some tree-shrouded pagodas. The two tanks rolled along between my platoon and the remainder of the Company, their guns barking at intervals. In front of the tanks crept a wave of fire as the artillery barrage lifted and dropped again deeper into the village.

We stepped over the bodies of Japs who had fallen trying to escape the battering. They lay like felled logs in a welter of torn scrub, broken plaster and stone – still forms in faded khaki and green. Strewn everywhere were shattered rifles and belts of machine-gun cartridges and grenades, helmets and blood-stained packs and equipment.

Squashed flat, their shaven heads pulped in the shifting dust, lay the bleeding figures of two orange-robed Burmese monks crushed under the shattered ruins of their temples' guardian Chinthis. One of my sections bombed the bunker with phosphorous grenades and the occupants scrambled out screaming, burning alive. Sten guns splattered: the screaming stopped. Sanity seemed to vanish in the din.

We swung left towards Sindat, snap-shooting at a crowd of Japanese. Some of them were carrying wounded comrades on their backs and running for the shelter of the village trees.

The platoon went in after them.

"Spread out! Spread out! Don't bunch!"

Dick was standing with legs apart, shouting, pointing to the offending groups of men with the muzzle of his rifle.

The other platoons were nowhere to be seen. We didn't look for them. We moved forward a few yards at a time systematically burning every building in sight. Enemy troops were running hither and thither to escape the flaming bamboo buildings falling in on their trenches and dugouts. We shot them down.

We went on slowly, carefully, each man covering his mates to right and left, crouching, ducking, bombing and burning.

A Jap grenade burst at my feet and I felt the tiny fragments slash into the calves of my legs. There was a burning sensation under my left arm.

I yelped and dived for the ground. Feeling no further pain, I got up and remembered to put my helmet back on my head. I caught a glimpse of Smithie's scared face.

"It's OK. High fragmentation, no sweat. Let's get on."

The village narrowed and we could see the sunlight glinting on the river through the trees a hundred yards away to our left. There seemed to be no one else but us in that world of crackling flames and noise.

We stopped momentarily and got down under the sweating weight of our packs and equipment. Ten yards in front of us was a wall of flame, as trees burned and dusty bamboo buildings exploded like rifle shots in the searing heat. The smoke and whiffs of fumes from high explosive swam past us. I saw the burning figures of three Japanese moving awkwardly, with clumsy horrifying slowness, and watched them fall in smouldering bundles, screaming, beneath a collapsing building.

Through a gap in the trees we could see one of the tanks on fire in a clearing. I caught a glimpse of two of the crew crouching in the open and firing their Sten guns.

Corporal Hughes appeared, erect and shouting:

"This way, this way over here. There's a gap. Come on, come on."

The men seemed to be suddenly consumed with a vast black savagery. We got up whooping triumphantly, and charged through a narrow gap in the wall of flame.

Beyond the burning tank some Japs were falling back, turning to fire and bomb as they went. The platoon went after them in a solid scrum. Near the end of the village the Japs attempted to regroup.

We saw for the first time an anti-tank gun. Two diminutive Japs in full equipment were swinging across the gigantic barrel to counter-balance the weight of the trail, which was being manhandled by what I assumed to be the gun-crew. There were half a dozen others covering them and snap-shooting at us. We rushed on them without pause, drunk with the intoxication of killing and destroying, our minds focused only on getting forward. When the blood lust faded seconds later there were Japanese lying all ways, some in shell craters their legs sticking out, others huddled against trees, most of them still, but a few jerking in horrible spasms, trying to get up, or turn over, or drag themselves on their hands. Their final attempt at defiance had been so bereft of the enemy's usual ferocity that I was awe-struck and incredulous. It had been almost too easy . . .

"Christ," I thought, "maybe the buggers were drugged!"

In the lull which followed, Peter Clark appeared, staggering blindly through the burning bushes and trees. Somewhere he had lost his pack, his helmet, his equipment, even his rifle. His general appearance held an incongruity which was appalling.

"Get up," he was shouting. "Get up. Keep moving forward!"

I ran back to him and pulled him to the ground beside me. There was blood on his face and he looked at me stupidly.

"This is it," I yelled, "the arse end of Sindat. What's happened. Where is everybody?"

Peter's face twisted in an agonised expression.

"Dead," he intoned. "They're all dead. My batman, the signal-lers, the FOO and his lot – they've all had it."

"What about Paddy and Sergeant O'Connor?" I asked incredu-lously.

"I saw Castles hit, and O'Connor too. Haven't seen their platoons since we first got into the village." His voice trailed off.

"God," I thought, "he's advanced half a bloody mile on his own."

"Christ, Pete," I said, "what were you trying to do? Capture Sindat single-handed?"

I told him to stay with Smith and went to the edge of the village where the platoon was frantically digging in. Everybody was angry and bewildered, when they realised that we were alone. I wondered if there were any Japs between us and the rest of the Company, or even if there was anyone left at all behind us.

Some of the wounded began calling for water. A Jap 75-mm kept slamming shells into the periphery of the wood along our front. We waited anxiously, wondering if the Japs would counter-attack.

Presently we heard the second tank moving up alongside us on the south side of the village. Every now and then its gun crashed and its machine-gun spluttered, as it backed into a blackened clump of bushes. The driver manoeuvred into a position immediately on the right of the platoon.

The counter-attack never came. We were still holding on to the end of the village in a thin green line half an hour later. The whizz-bangs were still coming over and their crashing explosions reverberated inside our heads. We managed to move the wounded into some Jap trenches which had overhead cover. We lay as though the noise of the Jap guns was beating us into the ground.

And then occurred one of those incidents which sometimes gave our particular war such an unreal quality. A Japanese in full equipment walked out of the splintered wreckage of the village behind us. He ambled straight through us and out into the sunlit fields beyond. It was as though we had watched an apparition.

Bullard was lying in a depression behind a blackened log. I could see him clearly, his face expressionless, his old pipe with the black insulation tape round the stem clamped in his mouth. He presented my picture of the immortal British soldier – quiet, unflinching, a sullen bull of a man, tough, kind, honest, harsh of speech. The battle-drunk Jap literally stepped over the tree-trunk, looking down at Bullard as he did so. I watched Bullard do a classical 'double-take' and then hurriedly raise himself to one knee. He brought up his rifle and I heard him shout above the racketing noise.

"Hey, Tojo!"

There was a sudden loud crash as another shell landed and the Jap disappeared before our eyes – blasted into a litter of flesh and cloth and leather.

I conferred with Peter, who seemed to have recovered himself a bit. He agreed to my suggestion that we should send a runner back through the village to try to get some orders for us. We had been unable to raise a squeak on our wireless. I sent Ernie Morrisroe, who gave the 'thumbs-up' and loped off.

A bit later Peter thought of trying to contact Battalion HQ through the tank radio. He called Bullard over and sent him off to try it. We watched Bull walk out of the comparative shelter of the trees. He was ten yards away from the tank when several shells dropped around it. We all cowered down under a shower of dust and débris. When we looked up again Bull had reached the tank and was struggling with the telephone contraption behind the right-hand track. He had the set in his hand and had begun winding the handle to alert the crew, when a fresh salvo of shells landed. The explosions blew him over backwards. The blast lifted him five yards, turning him completely round to face us. Tracer bullets were bouncing off the tank turret. Then Bull began to crawl towards us on all fours, and we could hear him cursing blue murder. Unceremoniously we dragged him back by the pack straps. He was yelling obscenities I had never heard before in a mixture of English, Hindustani and Chinese. His trousers were in rags and his left leg twisted and bloody.

When Ernie came back he spoke to Peter, who looked none too pleased. He turned and shouted to me above the din:

"Get the men together; we've been ordered back."

There was no need for a tactical withdrawal – we were not in contact – so everyone just got up and walked away. Peter suggested spiking the Jap gun, since it was far too unwieldy to take with us. Personally I had no idea how one went about these things. We packed the barrel with bloodstained shirts, stones and clods of earth and rammed them all down with a thick bamboo. Then we hauled the piece around and Peter slammed a shell into the breach. After attaching a piece of signal cable to the firing mechanism, we withdrew after the others. We got under cover and I put my hands over my ears. Peter yanked the cable and I closed my eyes . . . Nothing happened. Peter swore and was about to go back to the gun, when there was a titanic explosion. Never had we experienced such a deafening, nerve-shattering sound.

When we finally recovered our senses, we realised that the small dump of aummunition beside the gun, which most of us had given a wide berth since the shelling had started, was no more. One of the whizz-bang shells must have landed slap in the middle of it. Had that happened five minutes earlier, every man-jack of us would have been rags and bones on the Sindat tree stumps. We got out of there fast after that and the tank came with us. Some way back we stopped and picked up the crew of the other tank, two of whom were badly burned. The officer looked pale and shaken, but his voice was calm.

"Christ!" he said: "I didn't realise you lot were still out there. What's happened?"

"It's a washout," Peter told him; "We've been ordered to withdraw."

When we reached the other end of the village we found the CO and some of his defence platoon. He was directing 'C' Company who were busy carrying casualties across the open ground towards our erstwhile start-line near the derelict village. The Japs were still shelling the area. I wanted to take my lot back under cover of the river bank along the beach. Then I spotted John Margarson, who said that the Japs had the beach covered from beyond Sindat with a heavy machine-gun.

Before we had begun to withdraw I had found the Jap unit's battle flag fluttering forlornly on a bamboo pole. While we were waiting for orders from the CO to cross the paddyfields in our turn, I took the tattered rag out of my map pocket and stuck it on the end of my bayonet in a moment of defiance and, I suppose, of pride and personal vanity. After all, the bloodstained square of silk had been a symbol of the enemy unit's standing: losing it was a sign of defeat. We were retiring, but I was damned if I was not going to show everyone that we had been successful.

Beyond the derelict village we were met by the Frontier Force battalion going the other way. In their green canvas Foreign Legion headgear, with the neck curtains flapping, they were a very reassuring sight. We limped past them, feeling very proud and heroic.

"Where to, Johnny?" our men queried.

"Sindat *ko jao*, sahib," came the reply.

"It's all yours," we shouted. "You buckshees for Japani wallah."

The tall Pathans and Punjabis grinned, showing their white teeth. They trudged on towards the burning village.

The rest of our withdrawal was uneventful and I chatted with Peter on our way back to Alethaung. He was anxious about the Company Sergeant Major, 'Hookey' Walker, who had only recently returned to us. When Peter's HQ had run up against the Japanese machine-gun in Sindat, Hookey had put in a flanking attack all on his own. He had put the Jap gun out of action with grenades. The stretcher-bearers had found him lying wounded beside the dead gun-crew, clutching a Samurai sword. Peter told me he was going to write him up for a decoration.

The Regimental Aid Post in Alethaung was still in a tangle of confusion when we arrived in the village. I went immediately to try to find Bull and the others. I wanted to see them before they were evacuated. Bull was as game as ever, but confused from the effects of the morphine which he had been given.

"How goes it, old mate?" I asked him.

"I'll be all right, Guv," he answered. "Busty got it in the eyes; he's blind," he went on. "Paddy Castles don't look so good neither."

I tried to change the subject and told him about the Frontier Force consolidating Sindat, but he was unimpressed.

"How many went west from our mob?" he croaked.

"Only five," I told him. "And we went all the way, didn't we?"

"We were bloody lucky we got in right behind that barrage, or else we wouldn't have got halfway," he answered.

As I left him, I heard him muttering:

"Bleedin' tanks! Biggest balls-up . . ."

I found Sergeant Castles' stretcher and held a cigarette to his lips.

"Good old Paddy. You'll be all right now. Back over the river tonight and then . . . 'Chowringhee, here I come', eh?" He gazed at me, eyes sunken and staring with unbelieving intensity. His lips moved but no sound came. A short while later the jeep ambulances moved off, taking the wounded away, rolling westwards along the track into a blood-red sunset.

Terry Hodgson came over to my trenches in the morning to congratulate us. He told us that the Frontier Force had buried more than 90 dead Japanese in Sindat. The Brigadier was highly pleased with the way our attack had been carried home without the full benefit of the pre-arranged tank support. Not having seen Peter during the fight until the very end, I was too naïve to write up my report with sufficient flair to ensure a 'gong' for him. The truth is that nobody seemed to think about such things until it was too late. All we needed at the time was to eat so as not to starve, drink so as not to die of thirst, and to continue to exist, whole, unscathed, alive to the exact knowledge of reality.

I showed Terry our Japanese flag – he looked suitably

impressed but I could see that he was amused as well.

"You'll have to present that to the Regimental Museum," he told me.

"Hey, do you reckon that photo of us'll be in t'Carlisle paper?"

This from Billy Hughes. He was referring to the fact that when we had arrived back in Alethaung from Sindat, the previous afternoon, a war correspondent and photographer had mysteriously appeared. Seeing my pitifully small platoon dragging themselves along with me at their head like a standard bearer, the Jap battle flag on my bayoneted rifle, they had stopped us.

"You the officer?"

"Yes," I answered.

"Sit down on this bank. We'll get a picture of you." We sat and the picture was taken. We were torn between shyness and the glamour of an 'action' shot.

They asked us the name of our home paper. I never knew whether the photograph was published, but I still have the Jap flag – one of my few souvenirs of the war.

I learnt later that the flag of Japan represents, not the rising sun, but a chrysanthemum with 16 petals around a centre disc. The Order of the Chrysanthemum was the highest honour the Emperor could award to his loyal subjects.

NINETEEN

Mad Dogs and Englishmen

On the day after capturing Sindat we were ordered to reinforce the Indian battalion, which had consolidated only part of the village. My platoon was given the task of securing once again the bottle-necked eastern end of the village, which had been left unoccupied entirely for more than twenty-four hours, since we had withdrawn from it. We were not very pleased, in case this meant fighting twice for a bit of ground we need not have given up in the first place.

There were no incidents during the move across the paddy to Sindat, but when we entered the village and passed through the Indian positions, we could hear all too clearly the crump-crump of shell fire landing in the vicinity of our destination. Peter Clarke established the rest of 'B' Company on the left of the Frontier Force and I went on with my platoon.

One of the Frontier Force officers assured me that the shelling did not amount to much and had been only desultory for hours. We trudged on and Smithie muttered:

"Doosaltry, doosaltry; what the hell's that, then? One bloody shell's as good as ten in t'right place."

We approached the end of the village cautiously and found it deserted. A few shells kept dropping in the paddy beyond the wood, with a few overs into the river. These merely served as a spur to start us digging ourselves in furiously.

Half an hour later we were well below ground level and I wire-lessed a message to that effect to Peter. To my surprise I got through loud and clear the first time. With so many trees in the way I had only half expected to make any contact at all. Seconds later I had cause to curse the miraculous efficiency of my radio: the CO had left a message with Peter for me. We were to push on a thousand yards further along the river bank. The remainder of the

Battalion were on the point of moving up after us to occupy the eastern end of Sindat. I cursed the CO silently for being such an aggressive bastard.

I was reluctant to venture outside the sheltering trees and trenches onto the scrub-covered plain beyond. It looked decidedly unhealthy out there, and I spent a long time searching the ground.

A dense thicket of trees lay some three hundred yards away across the paddy, close to the river bank. Inland from that there was nothing much to be seen, but one could never tell. I decided to leave two Bren gunners and the 2-inch mortar detachment with Dick Florence at the edge of Sindat to cover us across the intervening bound to the thicket. I would plan the next step from there.

When I was satisfied that Dick's detachment could concentrate fire along the edge of the thicket at about ground level, then and only then, did I give the order for the move.

The meticulous care with which I had gone about the little job of placing the covering party had not gone unnoticed by the men. It was this kind of foresight, this preparedness, which I myself would have appreciated, nay demanded, had I been in their shoes.

I gave the lead to Bill Hughes. I had to keep a grip on myself so as not to sound too apologetic for selecting him just once more. With his usual cheerful and good-humoured acceptance, he turned to his section:

"Come on, Reid, me old son, tha can be scout. Let's get on with it then me lucky lads."

With a seeming casualness which belied their total alertness, the section began to move off, led by the oldest man in the Battalion. Reid made no secret of being in his middle forties. As he slouched forward ahead of the section, I heard him muttering at Corporal Hughes:

"Tha thinks I'm t' only Jap-bait in t' section, tha does."

How well I knew his feelings. When the 'finger is on you' at the sharp end of a war, it makes you wonder why it is that suddenly, for the first time in your life, you are the most popular, sought after, and well-known name around.

I had decided it would be safer to advance along the Irrawaddy beach. The lead section were thirty or forty yards away, when I followed with the platoon HQ and the riflemen of the other sections in single file.

It was mid-afternoon and a dead time in the tropics: the sun was hot on the back of our necks. All life seemed suspended on a breath; the river itself seemed to struggle languidly . . . mad dogs and Englishmen!

Reid was below the river bank at a point level with the thicket, when I saw him hesitate and begin moving again with the stealth of a stalking cat. He crouched low and then stopped suddenly, easing himself to the ground at the top of the sloping sand cliff. Signalling the others to close up and remain under cover, I joined Hughes' section below where Reid was lying. Instantly the wideawake, animal instinct of alarm consumed me. My sixth sense told me that danger was close. Even amongst the veterans in Hughes' section I felt fear stirring. I sensed them straining for the slightest sound or movement, searching without being able to see.

Slowly I crawled to Reid's side. He didn't move at first, but seemed to be held hypnotised by some overpowering spell. I moved my boot against his and scratched, signalling urgently. He pointed soundlessly towards some scrub ten yards away and whispered:

"Japs."

At first my eyes would not focus properly. A second passed like a week, then something moved in the tangle of undergrowth. A beehive shape of interlaced branches and leaves about two feet high took form. Inside this I saw the head and shoulders of an enemy soldier in profile. The movement which had attracted my attention registered, with the other details, in a split second of time. The man had lifted a pot-shaped helmet with both hands from the rim of earth inside his camouflaged cage and placed it upon his head. I could see his face clearly: the cheek bones were high and well defined, though daubed with streaks and whirls of colour like Red Indian war paint. The magnificent camouflage effect would have done credit to a chameleon, but . . . the man had moved.

Those who snigger at the suggestion of being afraid and irrationally intimidated by the sight of a man in war paint may be unaware that modern man can still be affected by such ancient and savage techniques. Let me assure them that, in the circumstances I have described, I was – and profoundly so.

All thought of my platoon, of coherent rational thought, of further reconnaissance, disappeared. On reflex only, without realising that I had moved at all, I found my rifle at my shoulder, safety catch eased forward, tip of the foresight hovering behind the right ear of the Japanese. I felt my right index finger squeezing the trigger. Slowly, eagerly, coldly, with utter contempt and cruelly aware, I shot the man through the head.

The exploding cartridge slashed the silence of the sleeping afternoon. The pot-shaped helmet bounced against the basketwork above the foxhole, uncovering the bloody gore of human head . . . and then I leaped forward, running insanely towards my kill.

I must have taken five or six paces before the realisation dawned that there were many more Jap positions dug into the bushes all around me. More to the point, I was completely alone. Standing stock still, as if paralysed by events or slowly returning consciousness, I became aware of the crack and hiss of small-arms fire and the shriek of falling mortar bombs.

Streaming back towards Sindat, my men were running blindly for the shelter of the village. The Bren guns I had left there to cover our move along the river bank were hammering bursts into the thicket, spraying the scrub at my feet. Even then, for what seemed an age, I stood at the edge of the Japanese position screaming, the blood lust churning and pounding at my senses.

"Come back! Damn you, you stupid bastard. Come back!" Smithie screamed. Tears felt hot on my cheeks and salty on my lips, I plunged after the platoon as sanity returned with a rush.

Ten yards in front of me, on a narrow track which ran along the top of the river bank, a man rose as though out of the ground and stood, Bren at the hip. The gun bucked against the tenseness of his arms as he fired. Burst after burst zipped past me into the Japanese as I ran. I recognised Smith, the Number Two gunner from Bill Hughes' section. Even before I reached him, jinking madly, I knew that he was past caring for life, that he would continue to stand there firing to the end. This uncanny premonition coincided with the burst of gunfire which smashed into his chest and stomach. His legs sprawled out like a horse landing heavily after a jump; he sank on his splayed knees still fumbling blindly with the Bren magazine. Then his back arched convulsively and he flopped over and lay still.

Panic stricken, with bullets stitching patterns in the sand about my feet, I caught a glimpse of the platoon, bunched, stampeding, with twenty yards still to go, for the trenches in Sindat. Swerving down onto the undulating beach I ran far out, zig-zagging towards

the water. Near the river's edge and in line with the covering party,
I found a depression in the sand and slithered into it exhausted.

Smithie's voice came to me through the crackle of gun fire.

"There's smoke going down now – run for it when it thickens up.
Now, now, come on up, run, run!"

But I couldn't run any more . . . I stood up and began to walk,
staggering drunkenly towards the platoon, shouts clamouring
about my ears.

"Run, run, for Jesus' sake run . . ."

I fell into a trench beside Dick Florence. A minute later, I found
myself trying to address the Company Commander on the wireless
set. The task was beyond me. Dick grabbed the earphones and
pressel switch from me and rapped out some grid co-ordinates, his
dirty finger stabbing at an equally grubby fold of map.

"We'll have the guns onto that lot *ek dum*. Company Commander wants you to dig your heels in here."

"You can assure him," I muttered, "that I am too shagged to do
anything else."

In due course a Forward Observation Officer arrived and gave
the thicket full of Japanese an unholy shelling from a 25-pounder
battery. During this stonk John Margarson arrived with his
platoon. They slipped off their packs behind our trenches. Half a
minute later, almost before the shelling lifted, John led his men at
the run towards the Japanese, who were still firing random shots
through the smoke. We watched John's platoon until it disappeared
from view. The dull whoomp-whoomp of grenades and a few scattered rifle shots echoed back across the intervening paddy. Soon all
was silent and still once more.

Two walking wounded came back, closely followed by a group
carrying a man across their rifle barrels. It was Beswick, a man
from my home town, with whom I used to chat whenever I visited
John's headquarters. Slowly without any particular emotion, I
untied the piece of parachute silk which Beswick was wearing
round his neck and laid it across his face. He must have died
immediately he had been hit.

We saw Johnny walking back across the paddy. He was talking
animatedly to his men, a peculiar twisted expression on his brick-
coloured sweating face.

"There's at least seventy of the buggers over there, all shelled to bits. Christ! What a bloody mess! Can you beat it, the only bastard left in one piece put a burst through Beswick." I had a sudden idiotic desire to laugh – to titter weakly.

John gave some orders to his sergeant and then lay down beside me. He stretched out at full length and put his arm across his eyes, half covering his face. I heard him quoting softly to himself:

> He died on the sand at the water's edge where all sorrows meet.

His body relaxed and a long sigh escaped his lips. It was sundown. I sat up and spoke to him. He didn't answer. Without moving an inch from his original position, he had gone to sleep . . .

As the sun went down we listened to the howling and baying of jackals and starving scab-crusted dogs, which moved in to scavenge amongst the Japanese corpses in the thicket.

Smithie was unusually quiet for a long time when we crawled into the blanket-covered trench for our nightly smoke after stand-down.

Finally he told me that the men were upset and talking amongst themselves about the way I had behaved in the afternoon.

"What the hell had I been playing at?" Smithie wanted to know.

I hadn't had time to work things out myself – I was still confused and I couldn't get the picture out of my mind of the other Smith coming back to cover me out of the Jap ambush.

At first my reaction was childishly defensive.

"What the hell do you mean – *playing at?*" I almost shouted at him.

"Shooting that bloody, half-asleep Nip sentry, that's what!" he answered just as sharply, "and then expecting t' lads to follow you into that wood full of Japs nobody could see."

"Bollocks! You pissed off and left me . . . All of you," I went on pointedly, leaning forward toward him in the gloom and jabbing at him with my knuckles. "Only the killer has the right not to be killed in this bloody game."

It was the wrong thing to say and I knew it. He took me up on that.

"Smith went back, but he would probably have gone whether you had been there or not."

"What's that supposed to mean?"

"He'd had a letter from his mother – came up before we moved in here from Alethaung."

"So?" I asked.

"Both his brothers had bought it crossing the Rhine."

"What are you driving at?"

"Well, you know as well as I do that Smith was Number Two on that Bren gun in Billy's section."

"Yes?"

"He pleaded with Cheeseborough to let him take the gun before we went along the river this afternoon – I reckon young Smith was out for revenge or something. I do know that he wanted us to bump trouble – he told me so. I thought he was nuts! Now I know he was – poor sod!"

We sat in silence for a long time.

After a while he said:

"If Smith was out for revenge, what were you out for? The lads are saying you think we let you down today."

I took a deep draw at my cigarette.

"They say you ran out on the beach to draw the machine-guns off us when we scarpered."

"My God! They're a damn sight too naïve for their own good if they think that. You were all bunched up like a crowd of perishing recruits. One long burst from a Jap that could shoot straight would have done for the lot of you. Whatever I was or wasn't after this afternoon, I'm still too bloody clever to be caught showing my arse like that."

Smithie laughed grimly.

"That's my boy. I was beginning to think you had the bloody death wish – or else you were dying for a medal!" Smithie giggled again at his own joke.

He stopped suddenly, choosing his words hesitantly.

"Them lads have come a long way wi' you, boss – take 'em the rest of t' way, eh?"

Before I could think of an answer he left me alone in the platoon command post.

Later when I went the rounds with Sergeant Florence, the men in the trenches greeted me as usual.

"Everything all right here?"

"Sure boss, *thik hai*."

We exchanged trivialities in the hoarse whispers reserved for conversation in the forward areas at night.

I spoke to them all in turn – their friendly response and cheerful banter told me all I needed to know.

There is some deeply felt need in the human soul for a pack leader in times of stress. I had the Colonel; these men had me . . .

And thereby hangs the danger of the tribe.

TWENTY

"Clear that Hill"

The break-out from the bridgehead had begun. We pushed on again further eastward, parallel with the river. On 10th March at noon we linked up with a patrol from the 2nd British Division.

Occupying Kalewa, from which the Frontier Force had moved on, we found that our Brigade had been selected to spearhead the pursuit of the rapidly withdrawing enemy.

The Divisional Commander's plan was for two Brigades (32nd and 80th) to converge on Kyaukse from the north and north-west, while our Brigade (100th) carried out a wide encircling movement through Pyinti, with the object of capturing Wundwin on the railway line, sixty miles south of Mandalay.

The Battalion found itself relegated to a comparatively minor role in all this. Our fitness for the hectic dash, spearheaded by an armoured and motorised column, was very much in question and I doubt we could have done it, lame as we were at the time.

Instead of accompanying the main body of the Brigade we were sent out into rocky undulating country, interspersed with small villages, mango groves and scrub desert. Thus began a march which was to last more than three weeks.

The Battalion was punch-dunk, practically out on its feet and reduced to twenty per cent of its proper establishment.

Sometimes during the march the men were asleep on their feet, but they still kept moving. We just went on, somehow, following the man in front. When the column stopped, each man bumped blindly into the one in front and groaned awake, like shunting goods trucks on a crowded siding. In the vast plain around us there was no life, no movement. We hardly felt our feet: we moved our legs but they only answered the brain's messages slowly. On and on we went, numbed heads vaguely attached to our weary bodies, and

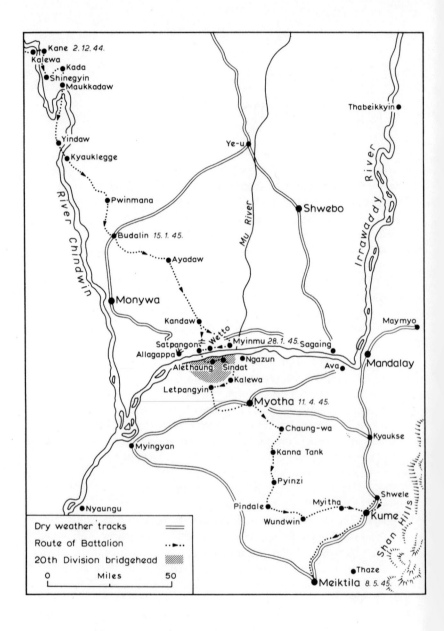

Kane *2. 12. 44.*
Kalewa
Kada
Shinegyin
Maukkadaw

Thabeikkyin

Yindaw
Kyauklegge

Ye-u

River Chindwin

Mu River

Irrawaddy River

Pwinmana

Budalin *15. 1. 45.*

Ayadaw

Shwebo

Monywa

Kandaw
Wetto
Satpangon
Myinmu *28. 1. 45.* Sagaing
Allagappa
Alethaung Sindat Ngazun
Ava
Letpangyin Kalewa

Maymyo

Mandalay

Myotha *11. 4. 45.*

Chaung-wa
Kyaukse

Kanna Tank

Myingyan

Pyinzi

Pindale
Myitha
Shwele
Nyaungu
Wundwin
Kume

Shan Hills

Thaze
Meiktila *8. 5. 45.*

Dry weather tracks ═══
Route of Battalion ∙▶∙
20th Division bridgehead ▨
0   Miles   50

when the orders came to halt we fell down and slept. Sentries were posted in pairs or threes to punch each other awake. The days came and went. Small parties of the enemy were encountered and several minor engagements were fought. In one of the earlier skirmishes Sergeant Winters was killed when he went out alone to bring in a wounded man.

Air photographs were passed round. The photographs had been taken several days earlier and dropped to us by the Indian Air Force. My platoon was ordered to reconnoitre the route. Scrutinising the prints carefully, we could see a camouflaged trench-system and bunker enplacements extending across the dry-weather track to the south. If they were occupied, I was to report back before first light when the march was scheduled to continue.

By 6 pm my platoon and I were several miles out into the 'blue', moving in straggled section columns. When the track divided upwards into hilly scrub, we followed the right hand one as instructed and came to a village under the lee of a steep rock-strewn hill. The village was empty and the track meandered on through and beyond. We walked on two miles more to our objective.

We advanced steadily, waiting, ready to drop to the ground. There were no shots. This was too right – too quiet. It stank. We advanced some more: it was dark now and we were strung out further and further to present as small a target as possible. The mounds on either side of the track appeared suddenly . . . we were there! With relief of nervous tension we flung ourselves down, scared.

Billy Hughes and Jock came with me for a closer look. Terrified of the bulky shadows we converged on the first bunker. There were other positions sited in a half circle, facing the way we had come. They were all empty. We reported back.

At first light the Battalion moved out. My platoon was third in the vanguard company and the Intelligence Officer was up with the point platoon, checking the route axis with map and compass.

At the track fork where we had gone right the night before, the point platoon went left. I shouted across to the Company Commander:

"That bloody fool's going the wrong way."

Peter sent a runner forward and another to the CO, half a mile

behind. The column halted, then went on again . . . following the
same left fork . . .

The land began to rise and the scrub opened out into dusty undulating desert country. The vanguard shook out into open formation
and began to toil up a long steep rise towards the crest of a high hill,
over which the thin track disappeared into the sky beyond. Looking
back, the Battalion snaked out in powdery dust clouds for almost a
mile to where the water cart, jeep-ambulances, the 3-inch mortars, a
Jat machine-gun platoon and a jangling mule-loaded detachment of
mountain artillery, Kipling's 'Screw Guns', fetched up somewhere
near the rear of the column.

The air on the mountain-side was oven hot and still, and the sun
beat down from a cloudless sky.

A bullet cracked overhead, uncomfortably close. Sniper! We
couldn't locate him. Then enemy mortar bombs began to fall all
around. The sniper fire became very fierce and a damned sight too
accurate. We dropped in our tracks and crawled everywhere. The
CO came forward and blazed angrily at me:

"Did you reconnoitre this route?"

"No, Sir."

"Then why did you report that you had?"

I was about to explain when he shouted at me;

"Get that lot of yours off their backsides and clear that hill top at
once."

Without answering I stood up and ran towards my men.

"Come on! Up you get; follow me at the double!"

God! What a bloody nonsense! This was where we would get
ours – I was sure of it. I was impressed at the speed with which the
platoon got moving. They were no mugs: they knew it was safer
doing something than staying there anyway. Billy Hughes, his face
streaked with dirt and sweat, ran up alongside me. His eyes were
tired but calm, reflecting the quick 'balls-to-the-bastards' resilience
he had always shown.

"Get them into the ravine on the right, Billy – I'm going to ask
the Old Man for mortars and the mountain guns to shoot us in."

But the CO was ahead of me. He had already given the order and
waved me away irritably.

"Which way are you going?" he asked.

"Right flank up the ravine and then in at 90 degrees. Shoot us in with the mountain guns as well. And for Christ's sake keep the Japs busy while we get up there."

He nodded and turned on his heel. As I ran for the platoon, I heard him shouting orders and obscenities through the sound of bursting mortars and small-arms fire.

Panic-stricken mules were dashing here and there, and the 3-inch mortar platoon was hardly set for action before the first salvo from the Indian mountain guns smashed into the enemy position on the crest of the hill.

Our stomachs began to rumble, we felt wind up, there was a general reluctance to move from the comparative safety of the ravine. After I had briefed the men quickly, there was no time to lose. The Battalion was out in the open on the pitiless hillside, almost without cover, with the plunging-fire from the Japanese spraying down amongst them like a hose.

Up, up we went, gasping for breath, smoke from the bursting mortar bombs drifting across the ravine. All the way up I was like a demented lunatic, urging the men on, cursing, cajoling, sure that I was leading them into the last attack we would ever make. Ahead at last, two hundred yards away, up a steep gradient the ravine petered out. From there to the enemy bunkers on the crest was about one hundred and fifty yards. Looking back, we could see the Battalion dotted about like ants on the bare slope amongst the mushrooming smoke clouds of mortar explosions.

They would see it all, like spectators at a Battle School.

The platoon lay down in the sheltering gulley to re-group. They were ready. All that remained was for me to stand up first and walk forward.

I swore a foul oath and gave the order to fix bayonets. It was a waste of breath. They were ready, watching me. Waiting for me.

Smithie, Jock and Ernie Morrisroe eyed me narrowly. Then I stood up . . .

The earth around the Jap bunkers erupted in crashing explosions. We broke into a trot, a run. A mad screaming and yelling burst from us. The barrage lifted. We leaped amongst the Jap bunkers and the fox-holes on the peak of the mountain. Smoke-bomb fins stuck up from the ground. Japanese corpses and pieces of bodies lay amongst discarded packs, helmets and ration tins. Ammunition belts and empty clips, spades and grenades were strewn amongst the debris of a hurriedly evacuated position. The Jap garrison, such as it was, had gone. His spoor, split-toed foot-prints in the dust, led away southwards over the crest of the hill into the empty scrubland beyond . . .

TWENTY-ONE

"Your Next Objective Is..."

From Myotha our Brigade struck south-east towards Pyinzi, and Pindale. Speed was the keynote, both to prevent the Japs from rallying and to give us time before the monsoon broke in June for the final advance to Rangoon. The Japs were confused and our various brigades played havoc amongst their lines of communication, spreading consternation among the enemy administrative centres, depots and dumps and his command and supply systems. Tough and forever determined, the enemy held on in every village, fighting stubbornly, clinging to the last. We heard of considerable numbers of Japanese trying to escape the rapidly closing trap as they rallied from the north and west. The Battalion plodded on in the intolerable heat which seemed to have reached its 'stoking up' height, presaging the oncoming monsoon weather. The blinding, suffocating, glaring pressure of heat came down about one's head and shoulders like a heavy weight. Legs and backs strained against the thin, tough material of our faded green uniforms. Dark, damp stains spread across the more permanent marks where constant perspiring left salt-dried white fringes.

The land across which we marched was barren, stony, dry soil and scattered savanna baking under the sun. The advance was a steady forced march with urgent demands from above to the divisions, the brigades, the battalions: "Keep up the pressure. Don't halt. Go on. Keep moving. Your next objective is..."

Some of the bamboo bashas we passed had been reduced to piles of black ash lying on the scorched earth, undisturbed in the sullen, windless heat. Trees around wrecked villages were shorn of branches and leaves, broken and blackened by fire. Only the Pongyi Kyaungs remained more or less intact. One felt the coldness of death in the alabaster images of the Buddha, whose face seemed to frown down on us deliberately – strong and malignant. When we did stop briefly for life-giving tea and shade, the atmosphere within the pagoda precincts seemed to be flooded with evil and with the musty smell left by the previous occupants, the Japanese.

In the distance, far to the east, beyond the eternal purple plain, rose the hazy outline of low jungle-covered hills, their shape almost lost in the brilliant turquoise vastness of the sky. They seemed little more than the pale stroke of a brush against the immaculate blue. There, far away, the Shan hills beckoned to the retreating Japanese. Behind us across the miles of dust tracks the procession of war rolled night and day – tanks, guns, jeeps, trucks ambulances. Among all these, choking and stumbling in the dust clouds, cursing the heat and the rumbling tracks and wheels, came the filthy veterans of British and Indian infantry.

Somewhere before Chaung-wa we marched like sleepwalkers all night, entering the village with the early morning sunlight.

There by the side of the dusty track stood a few dozen young, fit-looking men in blocked bush-hats, with clean pugries and immaculate olive-green battle dresses, some with creases in the trousers. These were reinforcements who had recently been flown in to a bush airstrip further north and transported by truck to meet us here. They stood watching as the tattered Battalion shambled silently by. The awed, preposterous expressions of disbelief on their faces told us more than anything else what ragged deadbeats we looked. More to the point, our appearance must have scared the pants off these newly joined 'rookies'.

My platoon dug themselves in to a corner of the Battalion perimeter on a stone-covered knoll.

Smith came over holding a steaming mug out to me.

"Char, boss?"

Stripped to the waist I sat on a mound of spoil near the entrance to a dug-out and watched the men moving about. Most of them were in 'bare buff' – boots, socks, grimy green cotton shorts and bush-hats, the sweat standing on their brown bodies and trickling down their arms.

This was to be my last bivouac with them. Within hours I found that I had been promoted to command a resuscitated 'D' Company composed mostly of the reinforcement draft. Finnegan was CSM. Chalky White and Spike Adams were promoted as platoon sergeants and Smithie, together with a sprinkling of old hands, was posted to help me get things into shape. We could only manage to make up two platoons but the men were fresh and looked keen enough. The platoon officers were Jock Walker and Harry Scholes, straight up from an Indian OCTU. The latter had been at school with me and, like myself, he had served in the RAF in the early days of the war and been invalided out. That we should meet again like this was an absurd coincidence and confirmed my deepening belief in fortuitism.

In April we were in Kume astride the all-weather Mandalay-Rangoon road. We had converted the large village into a stronghold from which to continue operations against the Japanese. They were attempting to disorganise the lines of communication and get across the road to escape into the Shan hills to the east.

Whilst operating from a patrol base several miles east of Kume, my Company was blooded gently in a series of fumbling little skirmishes against enemy foraging parties. For me, it was a nerve-racking period. I was intolerant of the lack of experience of the platoon commanders and their men, and impatient of the constant wet-nursing they required, faced with even the simplest tasks.

For several days we were relieved from patrol activities and took up residence in an old rice-mill on the outskirts of Kume. I found myself turning inwards upon myself more and more, introspective, constantly dreading the shrilling of the field telephone, which inevitably demanded fresh effort away from the modest luxury of our billet. I could have enjoyed long periods of uninterrupted sleep which, I noticed, my platoon commanders did. But I couldn't relax under the unaccustomed roof and the build-up of anxiety.

Twin pagodas in the centre of Kume housed the Battalion HQ and the Regimental Aid Post. I had begun to visit the latter, intending to discuss my nervous condition with Doc Protheroe, the Medical Officer, but I couldn't bring myself to it. I left him each time, consciously aware that my attempts at casual conversation had brought a concerned look into his eyes.

Passing the Battalion Command Post with a side-long glance at the place, I saw David, the Adjutant, busy about some mysterious task as usual. I moved on hurriedly, not wishing to talk to anyone, hoping to pass unnoticed. David raised his eyes from the talc, over which he had seemed to be absorbed, and shouted:

"Ken! Just the man I want. Come over here, will you?"

To one of his signallers he said:

"Evans, bring my haversack and two mugs."

I walked over to him. My heart skipped a beat. I doubted if my nervous system would stand it if he ordered me out with the Company again . . .

TWENTY-TWO

Go Home, Tojo

Ten miles south of Kume down the Rangoon road, like a long and rather sluggish worm, my Company wheeled to the east and fanned out in open formation towards the foothills of the Shan States.

It was nearly midday when Harry halted his platoon short of a low rise where the track bent its monotonous passage round some low brush. I found him leaning against a rock, his bush-hat pushed back on his fair hair and his rifle laid with easy casualness in the crook of his left arm.

"Right!" I said briefly, "we'll recce from the top of this rise. Where's Walker?"

"I think he's coming now," Harry answered and nodded towards the drifting dust where the other platoon had scrambled down the bank of a raw gully on our right.

Rubbing tenderly at smarting eyes, wiping weird patterns across his pink, dust-coated face, Walker appeared, grinning amiably. He was a nice-looking lad of about nineteen, with an enormous crop of ginger hair.

"Your platoon all right, Hookey?"

"Absolutely all right, sir – just a bit dusty."

"Right, let's take a look."

Turning to Smith I jerked my thumb upwards.

"Keep your eyes skinned, Smudge."

The miniature plateau, an area of barren, stony, dry sand and scattered scrub, baked gently under the noonday sun.

Silently I examined the prospect before us for some time.

The landscape was still, empty, naked in the searing heat. The track ran due east, a dull ribbon of silver sand, disappearing faintly into the bush-clad hills in the distance.

On all sides the open ground, hard-baked stretches of cracking

soil and brown grass, stretched away to the skyline. Here and there
the landscape was broken by shallow depressions and amongst
fringes of trees lay isolated villages with the inevitable white pagoda
umbrellas, glinting ethereal shapes, little more than pale smudges
on the vast plain.

An uncanny, half-fearful, cautious alertness, that always held me
in such circumstances, came over me. It was always the same, no
matter how often one had done it before. A unique physical and
mental tension – an instinctive knowledge, inexplicable but definite
– told me that the emptiness before us held the enemy.

"Right! We're aiming for those foothills before dark. We'll find a
place to hole up before last light and go for the ambush position as
soon as it's daylight tomorrow. From here on keep the men on top
alertness. Move in section bounds. Your platoon leading, Harry.
Any questions?"

"I suppose they could spot us easily from those hills, no matter
how we move, eh?" Harry queried.

"Sure they could, if we make enough dust. So don't. Move
slowly. Use all the depressions and cover you can find, keeping well
south of the track."

"Right!" They both said in unison.

"This is the part I want you really to concentrate on, getting
across this scrub. Even a couple of starving Japs with a machine-
gun could make quite a mess of things long before we get to those
hills. That's where his main positions are supposed to be."

We walked down off the stone-scattered ground of the low
mound. As the platoons began to move off, Smithie came and stood
by me as I filled my pipe.

"Do you think they'll have a bash at us on the way, boss?" he
asked, squinting into the distance.

"They're finished, and they must know it; just waiting to find
out which day it'll happen. What does he do when he's in that
sort of fix? You know better than most. He tries to sort somebody out, before going to meet his ancestors. The nearest somebody happens to be us."

Smithie's face became suddenly sombre.

I turned to Jones, the signaller, attached to my Company from
Battalion. He, like many signallers in the Fourteenth Army,
spoke fluent Welsh. This was an invaluable aid to security, when

for reasons of speed one wished to send messages in clear.

"That wireless net OK?"

Jones nodded.

"*Thik hai*, sir."

"Keep it open," I told him. "I want to know when we finally get out of range of the Battalion. Never mind the Morse; keep on speech. By the time the Japs translate your heathen lingo, it'll be Christmas. Keep talking to your mate back there all the time. Understood?"

The Welsh signaller nodded again, grinning.

The plain was silent and the sun bore fiercely on our necks. Small dust-clouds eddied round our boots. Twice in the next hour we stopped to scan the scrub through binoculars. At about two o'clock in the afternoon we came to a dried-up watercourse running at right angles to the axis of our advance. The chaung was smooth and gleamed whitely in the glare of the afternoon sun. The platoons had changed 'point'.

I watched Walker pause, examining something in the sand. Suddenly turning, he gestured towards us. Running diagonally across the tracks his platoon had made in the river bed were footprints which showed the split-toed unmistakable design of the Japanese patrol boot.

Half a minute later I saw Walker side-step and crouch behind a boulder near the top of the bank. Beyond him, not twenty yards from the chaung, near where Walker's leading section had gone to ground, three Japanese soldiers ran across a clearing into some scrub.

Firing broke out from the leading section and then we saw them run forward and disappear into the bushes. Seconds later there came the sound of grenades exploding. A Jap came zig-zagging out of the scrub. He stumbled down the bank twenty yards to the left of Walker's rear section and regained his feet as he hit the floor of the chaung. He was dressed in jungle green with a neat pack on his back and a camouflaged pot-shaped helmet lay low against his neck. Turning clumsily in the sand he struck a grenade against a rock to prime it and swung back his arm. Corporal Winstanley saw him just in time and raked the man with a continuous long burst from his Sten. The Jap collapsed, the grenade exploded a yard from his body.

Walker re-appeared and signalled us to him. He showed us six Japanese corpses in the bushes.

"Better send some patrols up and down the chaung, Hookey, and work another one forward through the scrub where it can see ahead."

Walker looked shocked and slightly dazed after his skirmish.

"Righto," he said. Then as an afterthought:

"Christ, I could do with a shit."

We kept the patrols going to the south and north for the next hour, but they found no further sign of the enemy.

We reported our progress to Battalion, who gave us 'Roger out' faintly. An hour later, with Harry's platoon in the lead again, we came upon another chaung. Down they went and then up the far bank. As Harry's lead section cleared the slope, a long burst of machine-gun fire split the silence. I ran forward with Company HQ. We were dimly aware of a screaming fusilade of bullets above our heads as we took cover behind a low bund. I heard Sergeant Adams shouting to his 2-inch mortar man to get some smoke down, but nothing happened; then Spike's voice again, anguished and incredulous, as though hardly believing the evidence of his senses:

"He's thrown his flaming bombs away!"

A grenade exploded, and another – and another.

I heard Finnegan shouting:

"Rapid fire!"

Another machine-gun opened up from somewhere to the right and traversed the bund inches above our heads. The frantic rapid drubbing of the Brens covered Harry and his lead section back across the chaung to us.

Smith cursed vilely behind me.

"The buggers have mucked off."

In one solid scrum Walker's platoon had turned on their heels and were running clumsily back from the bund through the scrub. The second Jap gun had the rest of us almost in enfilade.

Harry flung down near me.

"Jesus! Nearly walked on top of the buggers."

"Get back after Walker," I shouted at him. "Leave two Brens with me: we'll cover you out."

Bullets whistled and zipped about the bund, thudding and digging with deadly intensity into the earth and rock. Ricochets screamed off the stones and boulders. Heads low, hugging the earth, we began to give ground.

"Where are the damned things? Where are they?" We couldn't see the muzzle flashes from the enemy's guns or locate his exact position. We could only judge his dispositions from the sounds.

Walker appeared on all fours pushing aside the roots and thorn bushes behind me.

"Where's your bloody platoon?" I shouted.

"Adams managed to stop 'em about a hundred yards back," he gasped.

"Damn and blast them," I yelled at him. "Go back and get your bloody mortar going."

Soon after we heard the crump-crump of bombs and the sound of Harry's men panting as they crawled away flat on their faces.

"Thin out, thin out! Back two hundred yards. Move, move!"

There came the soft sough-sough of Jap spring grenades and their firework explosions; but we were soon out of range. At length we lay listening, shivering with fright and dripping with sweat, behind a sheltering knoll. The Jap guns had stopped.

Three more times during what remained of the afternoon we tried to move round the southern flank of the hidden Japanese. Not until it was almost dark did it finally occur to me that the enemy had a thinly held line of interlocking posts in a wide crescent across our axis of advance. It must have covered a frontage of at least two miles. Our objective was many miles beyond that line. There was still far more fight in the Japs than we had bargained for.

Finding a suitable place we scraped out a rough defensive triangle with our entrenching tools and settled down anxiously for the long night ahead.

Corporal Peaker, my medical orderly, arranged his First Aid box by the side of my trench.

We were roughly thirteen or fourteen miles south-east of the Battalion position and about seven or eight miles east of the motor road. We had four wounded on our hands.

"How about it, George? Think you could get the wounded back to the road?"

Peaker looked up sharply from his chores.

"Are you going on then?" he enquired. "What's the point of going up there to lay an ambush?" He gestured towards the faint outline of hills to the east. "Aren't there enough of the sods down here?"

"I'm going just the same. I'll take one platoon at first light. You'll need the other one as a carrying party."

George grinned and said:

"If ah can't see t' rest o' t' show, ah'll 'ave me money back."

As I gave out my orders in detail to the others, I felt my resolve cracking ominously. But I knew I would go on, nonetheless, to the final stupidity – the unavoidable end of obedience to orders.

The afternoon had brought a wincing and shrinking of my soul. The terror-packed moments of dread had pushed sheer unadulterated fear round and round the whirlpool of my mind. Suddenly I knew why the Japanese could contemplate the ultimate suicidal act: somehow it seemed no longer a remote possibility for me. The night hours seemed endless after that.

In the weird light of dawn Walker's platoon set off with Peaker and his wounded. The hot stifled night world began to breathe again with the first light of day. Harry and the CSM prepared the rest of the men for the move. They all appeared somnolent as they buckled on equipment and checked ammunition and grenades.

The ghosts which had haunted my thoughts through the dead hours crawled away unnoticed with daylight. I was once more in company with living men – veterans already – who knew and shared the true heart of fear. We set off in a wide south-eastern arc.

The time dragged by slowly and the hills grew nearer. The Japs had gone. The scrub gave way to areas of undulating ground and thick brush and finally jungle. We had long since moved out of wireless range of the Battalion. Advancing at a funeral pace we came to a stream at the bottom of a deep nullah with steep banks overgrown with jungle. Harry posted sentries, while the rest of us filled our water bottles and took long drinks. We scooped up the precious fluid in our salt-stained bush-hats and poured it over our heads and down the front of our shirts.

I was drinking deeply, standing up to my ankles in midstream. Harry appeared on top of the bank and signalled urgently, placing a finger across his lips. I joined him. Seconds later I found myself gazing into a circular hollow shaded by overhanging trees . . . at the inert forms of eight sleeping Japanese. Rifles and equipment piled neatly, the enemy soldiers rested, breathing deeply and quietly in attitudes of utter abandon. There was a tense and unnatural silence enveloping the hollow. Thick heat poured slantwise through the heavy branches of the trees and I could hear with vivid clarity the sound of a man drinking, twenty feet behind me.

I took out two grenades and laid them on the grass in front of my face. Already my mind was examining the situation, sorting, weighing, considering the factors and details. 'Do' this lot now? Must be an isolated party. Should get them all. Easy meat. Get a prisoner – then we can go back.

I glanced at Harry, quickly, fleetingly. His own grenades were in his hands.

"Now," I whispered.

The levers from the first two grenades pinged away like snapping elastic. A Jap stirred, raising himself on his elbow.

I watched the grenades roll to rest feet from where he lay. Kneeling, we hurled the other grenades in underhand lobs, watching them fall, with the Jap on his feet yelling.

The bombs exploded down in the hollow, raising dirty flame-shot balls of dust – one – two – three – four.

Harry's batman bulldozed through the bushes and raked the hollow below us with long bursts from his Sten.

"Leave one, you sod. Leave one, for Christ's sake," Harry bellowed.

The heap of bodies in the mushrooming smoke moved. A man struggled up, staggering and shrieking, blood in his eyes, his arms hanging loosely, messes of ragged cloth, red flesh and white bone —a horrid and gruesome animal thing lolloping upwards out of the hollow of slaughter.

The blind and broken figure staggered straight into the fire of Coward's gun, fell sideways and disappeared down the slope into the stream.

For a second or two a tremor of sheer panic hit me as another Japanese appeared not ten feet away. Then I saw he was holding his head in his hands, with blood creeping and trickling through the fingers, down the face and into the open neck of his shirt . . .

Bow-legged and stumbling, he glowered at us and his face held a stupid stare of courage. For a moment I expected him to fight, to spit and bite and tear at us in the way I had seen a wounded Japanese prisoner behave up the Ukhrul track—berserk, flinging four big

Tommies all ways before they had finally overpowered him. This one just slowly sank to the ground and remained motionless, while his arms were tied. He was obviously concussed badly from the blow on his head, where one of Coward's Sten bullets had parted his hair. Concussed or not, we were not taking any chances with him. While Finnegan placed a field-dressing on his head the Jap sat still, cross-legged, inscrutable, like a Buddha—slit eyes expressionless yet malignant. He farted loudly and often like an animal.

Without preamble we started back. I had the terrain mapped clearly in my mind. We marched westwards towards the Mandalay-Rangoon trunk, but with caution. Once when we had halted to eat on top of a rock-strewn shelf, we heard the noises of a large Japanese patrol making their way due east further down the ridge. Harry placed his hand over the Jap's mouth in alarm, whispering:

"Do you want this bugger inviting his mates for lunch?"

We devoured the last of our rations, rose and continued the march.

We were almost in sight of the road when Jones grabbed at my sleeve urgently:

"The CO, sir. He's on the radio. Wants your report, sir."

"Tell him we got a prisoner, otherwise nothing to report . . . *Nan tare* Roger," I answered curtly . . . "No, tell him I'm coming in up the road – should be there in about two hours."

As Jones spoke into the mouthpiece, the leading scout climbed up the banked shoulder of the road. We piled into the monsoon ditch which ran beside the crumbling cement surface and peered across the road and up and down. We smoked, relaxing thankfully: all seemed serene. Sixteen miles of sun-soaked scrub behind us, and beyond the Shan hills glowered. We glanced across the road again, the dying sun direct in our eyes. All of us heard the approaching footfall at the same time . . .

Steel-shod boots stamped out a rapid march step coming up from the south between the line of trees bordering the road. Striding out, right arm swinging, a rifle at the slope across his left shoulder, a tall white-bearded Sikh in turban and ragged khaki uniform came into view. The long straight road stretched empty behind him. We jumped out at him suddenly, threateningly. Quickly recovering from his surprise, he slammed to attention and formally saluted me. Someone relieved him of his rifle roughly and sent him sprawling in the roadway. He informed me that he had been held a prisoner by the Japanese. He had agreed to join one of their Jif brigades but had merely waited his chance to desert, hoping to march home to India. I didn't believe a word of it and had the Sikh tied up with the Japanese. I forget which one objected more strongly when they were tied together, but I was fascinated at the accuracy of the Sikh's spitting prowess.

We set off again, straggling northwards towards Kume, using the cover of the Monsoon ditch beside the road. A mile south of the Battalion perimeter I gave the order to form up in threes on the road itself.

Finnegan revelled in the job:

"Parade! Parade! Ten-shaaa! As yer weah! – Waken up there! Parade – Shaaa!"

It was getting dark when I gave the command myself:

"Buy the right – quick march!"

The Jap seemed indifferent; but the renegade Sikh regarded me incredulously. Finnegan looked back along the grinning files as they shambled after us, and his voice rose in a bellow:

"Pick 'em up there! Yer look like a frigging string of old pros coming back from VD 'orspital! Sing something, you 'orrible bastards!"

Surprisingly a man in the front file responded immediately in a shaky, untuneful tenor voice:

> I love a lassie,
> A bonnie black Madrasi;
> She's as black as the coals in fukkin' ell.

The others took up the tune, tossing the ribald words back defiantly at the crowding shadows:

> She's as black as fukkin' charcoal
> And she *saf karoes* her arsehole
> With a *tora tunda pani*
> From the well . . .

They were all singing it except for the Jap and the Sikh – stepping out, swinging along between the ghostly stillness of the trees and bushes which lined the road.

Nearing the outposts of the Battalion perimeter, marked by the looming silhouette of Kume, Finnegan broke into the Regimental

March, whistling it loudly. The others took it up, singing crazily:

> D' ye ken John Peel
> With his coat so grey . . .

And to that my Company swung into the Battalion position.

Battalion HQ had already packed when the Adjutant debriefed me after the patrol. David Kitchin seemed strangely jubilant.

"Christ! old boy, you had the whole Battalion on tenterhooks yesterday. They were waiting for the next score to come over the air all afternoon: it was like a bloody Test Match. Anyway, to hell with that! I've got news for you. They're flying us out of Burma to join another formation. Next stop, the Indian Fleshpots."

I came out of the Headquarters pagoda hardly daring to believe the evidence of my own ears.

Sergeant White squatted in the shadows outside, guarding our prisoners.

"What's to be done with these two?" he queried.

My deliberations were momentary only. Illimitable joy clouded my judgement: magnanimous in the extreme, I gave my answer.

"Don't like bloody traitors. So we'll keep Father Christmas," I said, indicating the Sikh. "But you can put a clean dressing on Tojo, give him a full water-bottle and some 'K' rations. Then kick his backside in the general direction of Tokyo."